Good Influence

Good
INFLUENCE

TEACHING THE WISDOM
OF ADULTHOOD

DANIEL R. HEISCHMAN

Morehouse Publishing
NEW YORK · HARRISBURG · DENVER

Morehouse Publishing
4775 Linglestown Road
Harrisburg, PA 17112

Morehouse Publishing
445 Fifth Avenue
New York, NY 10016

Morehouse Publishing is an imprint of Church Publishing Incorporated.

Cover design by Christina Hope
Interior design by Vicki K. Black

Library of Congress Cataloging-in-Publication Data
Heischman, Daniel R.
Good influence : teaching the wisdom of adulthood / Daniel R. Heischman.
        p.   cm.
Includes bibliographical references.
ISBN 978-0-8192-2363-0 (pbk.)
1. Church work with youth. 2. Influence (Psychology)—Religious aspects—Christianity. 3. Adulthood. 4. Conduct of life. I. Title.
BV4447.H377 2009
259'.2—dc22

                                                2009008006

Printed in the United States of America.

10 11 12 13 14   10 9 8 7 6 5 4 3

CONTENTS

ACKNOWLEDGMENTS

THIS BOOK HAS BEEN ruminating inside me for quite some time, and thus is the fruit of many years of thinking and experiencing. There are so many who have contributed richly to these ruminations, not the least of which are the countless students I have encountered, taught, and learned from over the years. It is due to them, and to whatever I have been able to perceive within them, that I have been able to develop more fully as an adult. (Young people have a way of doing that!)

Moreover, school—at whatever level—is where I have spent most of my working days, and my colleagues in those institutions have helped me to reap the rewards of being in daily contact with people of conviction, wisdom, and tireless dedication to the young people they are serving. Within those places of learning, I have also worked intensively over the years with a great many parents; their struggles, their unending concern for their sons and daughters, and their willingness to make tough decisions and hold their ground have taught me so much about how children grow best.

In particular, I wish to thank the Reverend Joseph Pace, a trusted friend, and Cynthia Shattuck, my editor at Church Publishing, for setting in motion the meetings that got me writing and for providing the support and encouragement that kept me going.

I owe so much to the people for whom I have worked over the years, who have given me both the freedom to pursue new challenges as well as their presence in time of need: headmasters Robin Lester at Trinity School and Mark Mullin and Vance Wilson at St. Albans School, and presidents Borden Painter and Jimmy Jones at Trinity College. No one could have asked for better leaders and mentors than I have experienced over the years.

I am very grateful for the guidance of the Reverend Roger Ferlo, Board President at the National Association of Episcopal Schools, who has encouraged me to complete this writing even in the midst of a busy work and travel schedule.

Finally, I wish to thank Sharon Daloz Parks, whose writings over the years have fueled my passion for guiding young people and understanding myself in the process; John Hanly, whose model of leadership of high school students came to my rescue each day I was Upper School Head at St. Albans; and the Reverend Will Billow, who taught me just how important it is to be able to laugh amid the most challenging of tasks and in the most frustrating of moments.

New York
April 2009

PREFACE

Krote ki gen granmoun, kabrit pa mouri nan kod.

Where there is a grownup, the goat doesn't get
strangled on its rope.

— *Creole Proverb*

THERE ARE SEVERAL inherent traps one can easily fall
into when writing about the nurturing of young people and
the best ways mature adults can do that important work.
How easy it is to appear self-righteous ("What is wrong
with parents and adults today?"), melancholy ("Why aren't
things like they used to be?"), severe ("It's time to get
tough!"), or, indeed, a mixture of all three. Readers might
find themselves thinking, "Why doesn't he just lighten up?"
or, "Does he really know what I have to go through, day
after day?" Whether one is a parent or a teacher, it is
tremendously demanding work to be shaping young people in a world where guidance, in whatever style it may be,
appears to be countercultural, not to mention a losing battle to be fighting.

That is why in this book we begin with ourselves, as adults, and consider what young people most need from us. In the pages that follow, the emphasis is less on how to raise your child, and more on how to be the best adult you can be for your children or students. That is a decidedly different and, in my view, much-needed focus; we are steering the conversation away from techniques and tips and toward virtues and dispositions, particularly as they relate to how we grown-ups live out our lives. Reframing the question in that way will, I believe, not only help us embrace our own adult tasks and perspectives, but will also allow young people to grow more fully into the adults they are meant to be—the goal that lurks beneath all of our efforts to do our best by them.

As I complete this book, an array of compelling literature is now being published that deals with the ways in which males (particularly those in the young adult phase of life) tend to put off the traditional tasks of adulthood, and the risks these postponements are creating for our common life. Likewise, as a society we are suffering the effects of what then President-elect Obama identified in December of 2008, when the full impact of the Madoff Ponzi scheme was becoming apparent, following upon the other financial collapses: "I think the American people are frustrated," he observed in a news conference, "because there is not a lot of adult supervision out there." Perhaps we are on the cusp of understanding, at last, the costs to our culture of the reluctance of adults to carry the mantle of adulthood, grim and demanding as it may appear to be from the quasi-adult sidelines. The need, as we are coming to understand, has to do not only with how we raise our children, but with how we live together as a society.

It is true that we may have to forsake some of our own self-indulgences and cravings to appear and act young. The times may call us to sacrifice, not only to trim our budgets but to build up our common life and speak to the deep needs of our children and students. In sacrificing, however,

I believe we will also discover a freedom to follow through on our convictions and allow that grown-up voice, at last, to speak up and be heard. As I hope to make clear, there are delights to be found in stepping up to the plate of adult-hood—far deeper gladness than our efforts to live vicariously through the young could ever offer—and those moments when we are able to set our adult seriousness aside and experience the child within us will be all the more satisfying and genuine.

In the trajectory I have outlined in the following pages, we are not asked simply to hunker down and get serious. Rather, we are challenged to discern the needs of the times, to reflect on the searchings of our children and students, and to draw upon the reservoir of images we possess, thus allowing us to set aside those childish ways of which St. Paul reminds us in 1 Corinthians. In doing so, we just may find the joy we have been searching for all along, a joy akin to finding our home and our place in the world. What's more, our children and students may be following us to that same place.

one

WHERE HAVE ALL THE GROWN-UPS GONE?

Living and Fostering the Grown-Up Life

There is nothing, believe me, more satisfying, more gratifying, than true adulthood. The process of becoming one is not inevitable. Its achievement is a difficult beauty, an intensely hard-won glory.

> — *Toni Morrison*
> *Commencement Address*
> *at Wellesley College (May 2004)*

A dignified adult life, with its heights and depths, protected by wisely kept secrets, once attracted children in such a way that they wanted to become adults. Now they see incoherent emptiness and chaos.

> — *Robert Bly*
> *in* The Sibling Society

FOR A NUMBER of years I served as the division head of an independent boys' high school in Washington, D.C., and among the many tasks I undertook was the routine but difficult notification of parents that their son had been either suspended or put on probation, due to a disciplinary problem or an issue of academic integrity. In solemn tones, and frequently over the telephone, I would preface the news by saying, "I have some bad news for you," and in most cases the parent already knew that something might be up. After sharing the news of the decision, I came to expect the invariable first question from the parent at the other end of the telephone: "Will this go on my son's record?"

In most cases, I was able to assure the parent that the school did not, as a policy, list disciplinary actions on the academic transcript that would be sent off to colleges. Moreover, with the passage of time and a clean record from that day forward, the official letter of probation or suspension would be removed from the student's file. It was comforting news to the parent still dealing with the shock and disappointment of this setback. However, as many times as I was able to reassure the parent, that initial question never failed to unsettle me: Was this, I would wonder, where we should begin? Is this where we should be focusing our care for the boy? Rather than ask about how his or her child was doing, or consider the lessons that might be learned from the whole experience, the parent went directly to the consequences. Would this be seen by the college admissions people? Would this hurt his future job prospects? Would seeing this on his record prejudice a future teacher against him? Somehow the internal life of the young man was taking a back seat to his external promotion in the world.

That particular type of telephone conversation, however, although common, was less frequent than another. With great regularity parents would call me to express their concern about how their son was doing in a particular class, on an athletic team, or with a group of friends: How come our son is not doing better in math class, and why did we not know about this before now? Why isn't our son getting more playing time on the soccer team? Why does teacher X not like him (as reflected in the poor grade he received on his recent paper)? Did I know what a bad influence one of their son's friends was having on him? In some cases, all the parent wanted me to do was listen; in other situations, there was a clear expectation that I should do something. After all, I was the one supposedly with the power to change things! In most cases, I would respond that I would be willing to pursue the problem, but I did need to tell the boy, or his teacher, or his coach, about our conversation. Suddenly things would take a very different turn; often the parent would say, "My son would be furious to know that I had called you!"

It is a familiar situation for many educators. In essence, parents wanted me to take action without their being implicated, largely for the reason that the child would be upset with mom or dad. Once again, the external factors—particularly the possibility that a son might be unhappy with the interference of his mother or father, that this would make him resent the parent—took precedence over how the boy was faring, and ignored the fact that emotional, moral, and spiritual growth often comes as a result of someone doing something to us or for us that we may not like them doing.

As I heard these concerns expressed with increasing frequency, I found myself wondering, "What does this say about us, as adults, in our contemporary world?" With a premium placed on the external affirmation and advancement of our children, along with the desire for our children to "like us," I began to conclude that there were some seismic shifts taking place in how we adults perceived ourselves as adults. We all seek to understand how our lives, and the lives of the young people we nurture, are being perceived by the external world; likewise, we all wish to experience respect and regard from the generation below us.

However, adulthood—particularly as it relates to the guidance of our children and students—is less about what *we* need than what *they* need. While parents may need to be popular with their child, the child needs parents to stand their ground. While parents may need to see the child always happy, the child needs to encounter experiences where disappointment and setback help her to learn and grow. While a parent may need to be perceived as youthful in appearance and temperament, a child needs that parent to be an adult.

There are many signs in our culture that our fundamental understanding of adulthood is changing. Whether it be the postponement of adulthood or the growing eagerness of adults to look younger and younger, we are clearly in the midst of a cultural shift that is changing the notion of full adulthood. Many of the traditional and principal indicators of adulthood—leaving home, getting a job, finding a spouse or partner—are increasingly being deferred.[1] Nowhere is this more clearly evident than in how we nurture the young. The love and care that young people feel from their parents and teachers is clearly abundant; the degree to which young people are listened to by their elders today is doubtlessly unparalleled. Yet there is simply too much of what we do, as adults, that is about getting our own needs met—whether it be the need to look and act young, or the need to live through our children—as opposed to looking out for the long-term good of those for whom we are caring.

This deficit in our understanding of what it means to be an adult stems from two principal assumptions about parent and child, student and teacher, the young and the old. First, our primary duty as adults is to care for our children in a particular manner, namely, to set our eyes on the long-range goal of raising and nurturing children, and that is to see that they become healthy, contributing, and independent people. Some of the ways in which we relate to young people in our contemporary culture, however, work against this goal. If we completely shield them from painful experiences, or create a web of constant dependency upon us as parents or teachers, we thwart the ultimate purposes for which we work with or raise children in the first place. As Robert Evans observes, "The ultimate point of parenting [and, I would add, teaching] is not to have children *like* us all of the time, but to have them *be like* us when they are raising their own children."[2] Frightening as that may sound, given that they may end up like us or that ultimately we must let them go to be adults in this world, our duty as true adults is to make that happen as best as we possibly can.

Second, caring and responsible guidance of young people depends upon understanding what they not only need, but are actively searching for in their growing-up years. It has, of course, to do with love, nurture, and warmth, with the development of self-esteem and a sense of accomplishment (with what we are fond of referring to as our children "experiencing success"). It must also involve something that our contemporary culture is less likely to understand or figure into the equation: the internal development of the young soul, and what images and influences feed into that soul. Likewise, as the following story shows us, it has to do with seeing beneath the surface of comments, actions, and moods that may deter us from being attentive to the growth and flourishing of that soul.

One Monday morning, I received a call from a father of one of our finest students who was troubled by a conversation he had had with his son over the weekend. As I had come to know Monday mornings as the "mop up" time for dealing with the fallout from the weekend parties, or the reporting of parent complaints about teachers or coaches, I was prepared as always for a long agenda of telephone conversations. This was a conversation, however, that stood out, both for its uniqueness and the depth to which it alluded.

Silas, the son in question, was a highly capable student, as were so many students in the high school where I was the principal. His academic performance was all the more notable because he had to balance his academic work with a demanding fencing schedule. Nationally ranked, Silas traveled a great deal to participate in fencing tournaments throughout the country and beyond, necessitating frequent absences from school. His ability not only to stay abreast of his academic commitments but to excel in them, given all that he had to juggle, was truly remarkable. I joined his parents in being tremendously proud of all that he had done, not to mention how he was also able to maintain a personable, responsive, and generous temperament through it all.

I could tell by the sound of his voice that Silas's father was rocked to the core by a remark his son made, which came out of the blue as they sat at the table for Sunday evening dinner. "I am wondering what I am really good at," he told his parents. Stunned by this announcement, his parents rushed to his defense: "What do you mean, what you are good at?" asked his mother. "Just look at all you do: you are a superb fencer, with a bright future ahead of you in college; you rank near the top of your class at school, you have lots of friends. You're good at a lot of things."

"I don't know," he replied. "I just wish I knew what I was good at."

Silas's parents had given him every opportunity he could possibly desire. They were attentive to him without smothering him. While they supported him by arranging travel plans for his busy schedule and worked closely with the school in arranging for him to complete work ahead of time or get back to schedule when he returned from a tournament, I did not find them to be the stereotypical "parents behind the star," pushing and advocating for their child while living their lives through their offspring's accomplishments. These were busy, interesting people in their own right, and they had regularly reminded Silas that it was his decision to continue with fencing; at any point, should he decide to give it up, they would be supportive of his decision.

Still, these competent and engaging parents were shaken by their son's observation. A question like that should not fit into the framework of a young man's life so filled with distinguished accomplishments. I found myself identifying deeply with the father as he asked me, "What could possibly bring on a comment like that?"

I responded, as I often did, by saying that it was likely there was some other question Silas was asking. Teenagers, particularly teenage boys, have a way of expressing their deepest longings and fears through symbolic actions and observations. Probably Silas was asking a more gut-level question about his identity through the mode that he knew best, performance. Like so many of the highly capable and sophisticated students in that school, it was easy to assume that, by virtue of his successful accomplishments and overall satisfaction with life, Silas was no longer a teenager, with all of the accompanying teenage doubts and questions. Given his ability to manage so many tasks in his life so successfully and given the articulate manner in which he could express himself, how easy it would be to assume that he might be beyond the adolescent struggle for a sense of self, a sense of soul.

"What am I really good at?" Like other questions that adolescents can ask, it is one that can go masquerading, these days, as something about external affirmation or a sense of self-worth. Its roots, I would contend, go much deeper, and challenge all of us to consider the fundamental needs not only of the young but of all human beings. No matter how sophisticated and accomplished our children or students can be, their inner life still needs to be nurtured and developed. They are still very much "works in progress" when it comes to a sense of self and understanding of the source and depth of the questions they ask of us. The understanding of that need, particularly in the young, and our response to it as adults is crucial to our fundamental understanding of our children and students. Call it the soul, call it identity, the center I am referring to has to do with what we can identify and claim about ourselves over and above what we do or how we are perceived. It is the inner core apart from performance, prestige, and praise—all things my highly adept students basked in during their high school careers. With admiring parents doting upon them, college coaches in hot pursuit of many of them, and distinguished academic records clearly reflecting their "gifted" status, it was so easy for many of these students, not to mention their parents and teachers, to ignore that dynamic, to sidestep the matter of the inner core. After all, with the external world telling them so much about who they were, why have need of what the inner self may be telling, or asking?

Another student, Simon, was struggling as a student. He found himself on and off academic probation during the first two years of high school. A warm, athletic, and jovial young man, Simon found the workload at this school a real struggle, and in spite of accommodations given to him by virtue of his diagnosis of Attention Deficit Hyperactive Disorder, he was finding some of the requirements—math and language, most particularly—to be daunting.

Going into his junior year—the year so many regard as the "make it or break it" year for entrance into a good college—Simon had embarked upon it with real resolve. When he had reported to me that he was planning to make "all A's" that year, I cautioned him to scale down his expectations, so as not to be disappointed. By mid-semester, he was floundering, and his parents were increasingly alarmed that Simon was not making the most of this crucial year. They requested, and we arranged, a conference with all of his teachers.

Joining us for that meeting were his tutors in math and Spanish, as well as his psychiatrist. With five teachers, two parents, three members of his "support team," and yours truly, it was quite an assemblage of adults, all sitting around in a circle, all of them talking about Simon. He was in attendance at this meeting, although he clearly was daunted by the turnout. What young person would not be, when all of the significant adults in your life had gathered in one room to talk about you, "the problem"?

Talk about him we did. Teachers pointed out his deficiencies, tutors asked questions about the level and nature of the homework he was receiving. That, in turn, made some of the teachers defensive. The psychiatrist sat quietly. Simon's father spoke at length about how he wanted Simon to experience some success this year, raising the issue of waiving some of the graduation requirements that stood in his way, and his mother's chief concern was Simon's self-esteem.

As the meeting went on, I felt increasingly impatient, as it seemed that we were talking too much *about* Simon and hardly enough *with* him. Moreover, not one of us had asked him either how he felt about all of this or what his opinion might be. At one point, I turned to him and said, "Simon, if I were in your shoes I would be pretty intimidated by this gathering, and I am wondering how you are reacting to all of this." Some of the adults in the room seemed strangely startled by my question, while others reacted as if it was a stroke of profundity. Simon smiled, I suspect in part because someone had, at least, noticed him. However, he did not have much to say. Father prodded him to speak up on his own behalf, but Simon's comments were short and clipped, confined to the occasional, "I don't know," or, "I guess so."

Toward the end of the meeting, I asked, as I routinely do in such problem situations, if this was the right school for Simon. Perhaps he would find more success and the demands more manageable at a less pressurized environment. Simon was quick to say how much he loved the school. Moreover, his parents would not entertain the possibility of leaving the school. "It is his home," they replied, yet I wondered if it was less a matter of being his home than the most powerful launching pad for the successful future they envisioned for their son.

Silas and Simon may seem to have been in different worlds. On the one hand, Silas had managed to find academic success and athletic distinction; he had put together for himself a challenging, full, and interesting life as a teenager. Simon, on the other hand, had not found a niche for himself, nor had he lived up to the obviously high expectations his parents had of him. Provided with all of the help and support a young person could possibly need—parents, tutors, a psychiatrist—he was not able to articulate what was going on inside of him, be it the presence of feelings of failure or of frustration with a system that was quickly labeling him an underachiever.

At second glance, however, Silas and Simon shared a common dilemma, one that put them in good company, not only with each other but with countless other young people of this generation. Life presents them with many obstacles, challenges, and baffling circumstances, and these situations produce a great amount of internal distress (as they do with all human beings). Yet these young people yearn to find an inner core or compass that not only would help them begin to understand themselves in times of distress, but would help them define and disentangle themselves from the web of performance, the need to be cool, and their anxiety about what the outside world thinks of them. The "core" of which I speak has a moral component, for it is the reservoir of our convictions, sense of commitment, and yearning for a better world. There is a spiritual component, in that it places the inner life of a young person within a larger, transcendent framework. Within the framework of my own faith tradition, it means that one is not only a performer, one is also—and more importantly—a child of God. It is also, however, the place that can identify and supply a yearning for the person we have not already arrived at being, a yearning so crucial to the growth and flourishing of young people. Whether it be a sense of understanding what Silas is "really good at," or a reservoir from which Simon could find the words to express what is stirring deep inside of him, it is this inner core where all of the voices and aspirations of one's life come together. It is, in essence, where the young person feels as "one."

The need to connect with themselves at this depth can go easily unnoticed by young people as well as by the significant adults in their lives. The inner core cannot develop in a vacuum, as it needs models of inspiration and admiration. Yet for so many young people, there is indeed a vacuum when it comes to finding those sources of inspiration. At their core, many young people are finding themselves starved for some notion of what they should be reaching toward and how they can get there. The adults in their lives, be they parents, teachers, or other mentors, do not see it as their role or do not have the resources to live up to the role that is required of us. Those of us who live in that realm called "adulthood" have, in the words of Gary Cross, "failed to create new and abiding understandings of being a grown-up"[3] that will both equip us for our own embracing of maturity as well as fuel the inspiration young people need for the adult road that lies ahead of them.

While I was a college chaplain, I frequently was asked by students about to face judicial boards—be it for social infractions or academic dishonesty—to accompany them to those hearings. Whether it was for cheating on a test or paper or flagrantly offensive behavior on campus, the college allowed for an adult to be with the student in the hearing, not as an official advocate but simply as a supportive presence. Whether or not students thought I might be able to provide some type of "divine interference," it was a fascinating change from being on the disciplinary end of such situations, as I was in the high school where I served.

Once the hearings were completed, I would ask the student how he or she felt. Quite frequently, the answer came in the form of, "That was not me they were speaking about." While the student might have admitted to the infraction, it was the experience of many that the collective assemblage of affidavits, witnesses, and questions about the incident in question did not get at their "core"—did not touch upon the essence of who they were as human beings. In fact, some of them maintained, it felt contrary to their "true" self. Hence, they felt that a distorted picture had emerged of them, spoken of in an open hearing, and it frustrated and embarrassed them. Those students feared that the part of themselves under disciplinary discussion would be seen as the sum total of who they were, and in such moments they were quick to assert that inner core representing the person they knew themselves to be over and above a single incident. They concluded, and concluded rightly, that they were "more" than the person being judged in the hearing.

That is the inner core, the "more," the sum total of which I speak. It is something we all seek, all need, over and above our ability or inability to perform, to meet expectations, or to receive external praise or blame. Sadly, however, it is the one dimension of the lives and worlds of young people that is most at risk in our culture today, in part because adults are not comprehending the need. The postponement of adulthood, the "belief that an adult can relate to a youth only by accentuating his or her own maturity"[4] or the living of one's own fantasies or ambitions through one's son or daughter, has left adults barely able to provide the models of adulthood that our young people so need. All of these factors may have resulted in a generation of "semi-adults," who may feel young and in touch, but it has left the young people in our midst bereft.

Madeline Levine, a clinical psychologist in California who has worked with young people for many years, speaks powerfully of the need for the development of what she refers to as an "internal home" in young people:

> What is an internal home? It clearly is not built of bricks and mortar, but of the psychological building blocks of self-liking, self-acceptance,

and self-management. It is the welcoming and restorative psychological structure that children need to construct in order to be at ease internally as well as out in the world. It is where kids—where all of us—retreat to when we need to "pull it together," "think it over," or just take care of ourselves.[5]

It is precisely this "internal home," as Levine refers to it, that she believes many young people lack. Much of the energy that might have gone into developing that core has been channeled into the drive for external recognition, the proliferation of awards and affirmations, and the appearance of sophisticated aloofness called "coolness." As the character of Fernando Lamas, played many years ago on *Saturday Night Live,* used to remind us, "It is not how you feel, but how you *look* that counts!" With attention focused solely on how the world out there perceives us, how can young people look inward? With the tendency of parents to solve problems for their children—thus leaving them in a state of perpetual dependency—how can young people develop problem-solving capabilities and learn from the school of hard knocks? With all of us basking in a culture of immediate gratification, how will we learn to view the long-term perspective? All of these factors work against the cultivation of that internal home, the very home that might have come to aid both Silas and Simon in their respective understandings of themselves. Our culture, and how we seek to "manage" young people, leaves many of them unable to speak out of the reservoir of self they need in order to navigate the challenges of living in our world today.

Sadly, this is not a problem that can be solved easily. Nor is our first tendency to begin to solve it the right one. For the solution to the problem, in my estimation, comes initially from another source. In our world of quick fixes and "tips" to help solve the problems at hand, our first inclination is to think that we must change young people—perhaps their habits, schedule, or external pressures—in order to develop that internal core. Perhaps we should offer academic courses in "inner coreship," and we could point to the most popular course offered at Harvard for undergraduates, one on happiness, to serve as tools to come to our—and their—aid. The symptom we see is indeed a culture of young people with highly underdeveloped internal cores. The deeper problem, however, lies not with young people, but with us adults—their parents, their teachers, their role models. Our understanding of ourselves as adults, I would maintain, is the place where we begin to foster a sense of the internal home that Levine speaks of so eloquently.

A colleague who once encouraged me to write a book then asked what I would write about. Given my background and experience, I said such a book most likely would be about education, or a theology of education. "What would you title the book?" he then asked. The response came out of my mouth before I could even think of an appropriate answer. "Adulthood," I said. Not surprisingly, my colleague was shocked. "What does that have to do with either theology or education?"

Everything, I would maintain. It is no surprise that, alongside the challenge for young people to find an internal coherence to their lives, we see so many adults desperate to stay young, not only in appearance but also in temperament, thus relinquishing the essential adult role of self-regulation. As young people struggle to speak from a place within themselves, so we see their elders struggling to speak of what it means to be an adult in terms of jobs, owning a home, raising a family, or being able to make decisions. While we admire so many young people performing at extraordinarily high levels—be it in the classroom, on the playing field, or in the artistic world—we also see their parents merging their own worlds with those of their sons or daughters. As the parent of a high-achieving student complained to me on the telephone, "We did not get Spanish." *We*? In other words, the adults in the lives of young people are not tending to that same inner core either, and therefore we are left with an alarming vacuum in that space we call adulthood.

We adults need to focus more on ourselves, as adults, if we are to provide young people with the rich internal life they need. What will *not* help them in their struggle to understand what it means to grow up is to see themselves reflected in the wants and needs of their parents or teachers. As the poet and educator Robert Bly put it some years ago, "The adult in our time is asked to reach his or her hand across the line and pull the youth into adulthood. That means of course that the adults will have to decide what genuine adulthood is."[6] To navigate this journey, young people need to see models of what it means to be an adult, and those models need to be less "in touch" with the world of youth and more distant from it.

That is no small task. Whether we are Baby Boomers or Generation Xers, the grown-ups of today view adulthood as something grave, heavy with responsibility, elusive, and distinctly un-youthful. Perhaps it is our reaction to the generation gap we experienced growing up, when our parents seemed so much "older" than we were; it could also be the increasing pull the media exerts toward youth. No doubt the decreasing amount of time we are able to spend with our children intensifies our need to feel we can relate to them. All of these factors and more contribute to the confusion we experience over what we are about as adults. Just as Silas and Simon are struggling to find words to speak out of their deepest longings and convictions, so the grown-up of today struggles to give shape—in word, attitude, and action—to what makes them different from the young.

Fortunately, young people are eager for us to assume such a role. As has been aptly pointed out about this generation of young people, they are eager for and receptive to the advice and help of their elders. Moreover, when asked who their heroes are, so many of them point not to civic leaders or athletes, but to the local hero—the parent, grandparent, or teacher who interacts with them on a daily basis. These are the people who genuinely mean something to the youth of today in a way that I believe our generation did not seek from their elders.

The crucial question is, can we respond to that invitation in a mature, indeed adult, manner? To point us in that direction, I draw upon five words that capture, in part, the attitudinal shifts we need to make toward an intentional and mature look at how adulthood must be better understood and grasped.

Differentiation. What are the distinguishing features of adulthood, as opposed to the youthful image and ideal that draws us away from it?

Dissatisfaction. In what ways do we find ourselves dissatisfied and frustrated in a world where fewer people are prepared or motivated to take on an adult role?

Duty. What are some of the adult responsibilities our children and students need to see us undertake, regardless of whether we are drawn to these responsibilities or not?

Difficulty. When we utter the words "adult," or "grown-up," what images come first to our minds? Do they come from our parents? What do we find most difficult to accept about them?

Delight. What are some of the true pleasures and delights to be found in embracing the adult role? How can we learn to enjoy that role?

While these five words may help clarify the direction we are to take, what follows in this book is an unusual and challenging path. We begin with perhaps the biggest challenge young people face today, developing that internal core. But rather than focusing on how to raise kids or teach students, what if we instead focused on cultivating a sense of how we parents, teachers, and mentors develop an adequate sense of ourselves as adults? Of course, we are not used to spending as much time as this book does on what it means to be an adult—including, as Toni Morrison reminds us, its elegance and beauty. That might be part of what makes it seem a less than appealing undertaking, yet I remember the words of one of my favorite authors, Sharon Daloz Parks: "Look hard at what you like. Look harder at what you don't like."[7] That mode of reflection not only gives us courage, but also speaks to the needs of young people. The two are intimately and—to many of us—alarmingly connected. Spelling out that sense of gravitas, that unfamiliar territory, is the task ahead of us. It is also the answer our young people most need from us now.

two

LANDING THE HELICOPTER

Reclaiming the Importance of Influence

There were no grown-ups in charge of the system.

—*Steven Pearlstein*
of the Washington Post,
describing the recent financial collapse,
on Meet the Press (*September 21, 2008*)

When I feel recognized and have a sense that you
understand how I am experiencing my experience,
I can find your limit setting tolerable and even a
relief.

—*Robert Kegan,*
The Evolving Self

IT IS A FASCINATING exercise to watch. College students, just getting out of class, reach for their cell phones to see if any messages were left for them during the last hour. Frequently this is followed by return calls as they begin crossing campus en route to the library or back to the residence hall. Given what we know of young people and how they rely heavily on their peers, we might assume that these calls are to friends or those with whom they are romantically involved. Instead, "Hi, Mom, I just got out of Psych class" may well be the greeting to the person at the other end of the telephone.

If a recent survey by Middlebury College is correct, the average undergraduate is calling mom or dad at least two times a day, and no doubt many students check in more often than that. Truly, our young people today are in touch with their parents in ways that could not have been imagined by many of us when we were in college. Not only is this something that parents have come to expect, but their sons and daughters seem to be willing participants in a trend toward heightened communication between the generations. No doubt some of this is due to our increasing sense of living in a fragile and dangerous world. In 2007, the National Association of Independent Schools, in its annual survey of parents as to the reasons they send their children to independent schools, found that safety—for the first time—topped this list of reasons, overtaking such factors as academic excellence, individual attention, or the assumption that a given school will get their sons or daughters into Harvard.[8] Ours is a society where we need to make contact with those we love on a regular basis—hence the frequently heard phrase, as passengers board an airplane, "Hi, honey, I am just getting on the plane." More than ever before, we seem to need to know where the other is—not so much for information's sake as for the assurance that all is well. The perils and perplexities of our world today, combined with the ease of technology, make what may have seemed excessive in the past almost a requirement for our growing need to be in touch. In many cases this intensified amount of communication may be viewed with pride by some parents, seeing it as a significant departure from the "gap" they experienced with their parents in their own teenaged years. Moreover, who would not be gratified by the need for one generation to be in touch with the other? Such reaching out and being in touch with the young seems like a refreshing and critical bridge to have crossed. We congratulate ourselves on the progress we have made in communicating with and hearing the young.

However, there are dangers inherent in our need to be constantly in touch with our children. One is that we may fool ourselves into thinking that we know more about them than we really do. I have often heard from parents a variation of the confident but deceiving statement, "My child tells me *everything!*" It assumes that frequency of communication leads to depth and comprehensiveness. For another, we are fostering a sense of greater dependency in our youth as problems that otherwise would have been sorted out by them on their own now are getting taken to the parental tribunal. For example, the question, "What courses should I be taking next semester?" can easily lure parents into thinking how needed they are and how strong communication is between parent and child. Instead, we adults need to be asking about our *own* needs and how those are being met through such intense communication. Are we judging our effectiveness as parents and mentors solely on the basis of being in touch? Do these daily tasks of checking in tend to assuage our worries about how we are doing with guiding young people? Likewise, are our own personal needs for closeness in some way satisfied through these mechanisms of communication with our children?

Giles was among the most responsible, conscientious, and well-meaning young men I have ever taught. He maintained a deep commitment to his studies, his involvement in the larger life of the school, and his loyalty to home and church. As I had often told his parents, they could take great pride in the young man they were nurturing along toward adulthood. His parents took their roles very seriously, in terms of regular communication with the school and attempting to understand the larger developmental issues of the boy they were raising. Yet, I also detected underneath the clear indicators of positive growth a sense of fragility. There seemed to me, as I spoke both with son and parents, a sense of impending danger; at any moment everything could spiral out of control. The extent to which they were involved with their son's life, as well as the vulnerability I sensed in the young man, gave me the impression that his developing roots were not as sturdy as one might hope.

One day I received a worried telephone call from Giles's mother, who informed me that she was on her way to the school and wanted to have a few minutes of my time when she arrived. When I asked her what the problem seemed to be, she informed me that she had just heard from Giles that he had received a B on his midterm grade in Calculus. Such a grade was unusual for Giles, and certainly not what his parents expected from him. Not only had the news caught his mom by surprise, but there was a clear note of panic in her voice. Given the importance of the eleventh grade year—in its intensity as well as importance for college admissions—and given the highly symbolic role that Calculus played in that pressure-filled year, the news carried with it more urgency than that of a grade received in another course at another time.

Only when Giles's mother arrived at school did I realize what had transpired. She was having her hair done at a local salon when her cell phone rang; it was Giles, informing her in an anguished voice of the news he had just heard about his math grade. Within minutes she was out of the salon chair, into her automobile, and on her cell phone to me, ultimately landing in my office to address the problem. Talk about a quick response, of being—as we are fond of saying these days—"all over" an issue!

I have no doubt that Giles's mother felt she was being responsible and responsive to her son's upsetting news and mood. Most parents today would prefer that their son or daughter would come to them as quickly as possible with such news, rather than—as I would have been tempted to do with my parents—keep it from them as long as possible. While Giles's mother seemed shaken by the news, I did not have a sense from her that, at the time, there were any other options for her than to act on this news as urgently as possible. She clearly felt she was doing the right thing, the natural thing, the only thing.

Yet I wonder about the long-term, unspoken impact this series of events had on Giles. If I read the situation correctly, she quickly plugged into Giles's sense of panic, responding in kind both to his youthful sense of calamity as well as his need to have something done immediately. Moreover, there seemed to be a curious absence of perspective. Could it possibly be the case that a B on a midterm grade did not warrant the sense of alarm that truly devastating news can and should elicit from us? Did dashing out of the salon chair and into my office provide Giles with an example of how to face news of setbacks? What did Giles learn not only about how his parents responded to his cries for help, but how problems that will inevitably be faced in the future should be dealt with? Had he learned that mom and dad will respond instantaneously to his sense of panic? If so, I wonder if that came at the expense of learning how to approach and perhaps deal with the problem himself, on his own time.

What I fear most is that through being constantly in touch with our young people we are producing *fusion* with the young, instead of instilling within them a sense of our *influence*. The sense of immediacy, the ease with which we can access the other, flies in the face of what I would like to call the lasting impact—what I would like to call influence—that adults can and need to have on young people. If a parent launches into action impulsively and irrationally whenever the cry for help comes, that parent is fusing with her or her child. Giving the child not only time to figure out a way to tackle the problem, but also the opportunity to search his or her own inner core for the important voices that will help solve that problem—asking, for example, "What would mom or dad do in this situation?"—is an example of influence. To recover that sense of influence, and what that means both to the adult and to the young, is perhaps the most essential, telling, and pivotal element in our efforts to guide and be of help to the next generation.

All of us are eager to be of influence with others. We need to teach, as Erik Erikson wrote, not only in the classroom but in the example of our lives. As he continues, "Every mature adult knows the satisfaction of explaining what is dear to him and of being understood by a groping mind."[9] We all seek to leave our mark in some fashion, so that others will not only have felt our impact, but that such an influence will make a difference to them. Parents are eager that what they most hope for in the lives of their children will in fact take place, that what they stand for and see as most important in life will rub off on their son or daughter. This impact will help their children not only to deal with the inevitable complexities of life, but indeed thrive in that life. So, too, teaching is, by nature, an idealistic profession: teachers believe that they can make a difference in the lives of their students, that not only what they teach but who they are as human beings will have a transformative effect on at least some of the students they interact with on a daily basis.

Many have been the times, in the schools where I have worked, that a prominent lawyer, doctor, politician, or business executive will come to the school as a guest lecturer in a class. Inevitably, I recall all of them coming away from those experiences with a sense that what they were doing that day, in sharing some of their expertise as well as the story of their personal commitments to their profession, truly mattered. Some of them, over the years, have spoken longingly in retrospect not only of how much that experience meant to them but how much they might like to teach a class on a regular basis, or even devote their whole working life to something that seemed to be of obvious or similar worth. As Erikson reminds us, there are few things more natural to us or more rewarding for us than to be teaching the next generation.

At the same time, there are few challenges more daunting than the prospect of seeking to have an influence in the lives of young people. Not only are the stakes high—we are talking about having an impact on the next generation!—but it is hard to know if what one has to offer young people is something they will welcome. When I was the chaplain of Trinity School in New York we had a fund for chapel speakers, and I decided I would get some of the biggest preaching names in New York to come and show off their homiletical talents to our students in chapel. So, in would come golden-throated preachers from highly endowed and powerful parishes, some of them larger than life personalities used to preaching before attentive and astute throngs. Strangely enough, though, many of them would come into my office prior to the chapel service seeming anxious or nervous. Preaching to the rich and powerful in New York was easy compared to the task of trying to reach teenagers who, in their facial expressions or the manner in which they were sitting in the pew, would give the impression that they had absolutely no interest in what you had to say. I even remember trying to get one of the great gurus of positive thinking to come to preach in our chapel, year after year, but he would decline each time. Finally, I said to him, "Should I stop nagging you about preaching for us?" He responded, "I just don't feel like I have what it takes to preach to young people."

Being a parent or a teacher is always an exercise in humility—invariably what you "preach" will come back to you at some point, often by the child pointing out the discrepancy between what you say and what you actually do. The young have a particular capacity to identify hypocrisy in their elders. Moreover, in a world of competing truth claims, how can we parents and teachers be certain that what we believe is worth seeking to impress upon young people? "Who am I," the adult asks, "to think I can impose my beliefs onto my children or students? Will they even want to listen to what I might say?" Indeed, I am convinced that a part of the desire some parents have had in recent decades to allow their son or daughter to choose their own values as they grow is a way to sidestep the ambivalence they themselves might feel about the quality and enduring value of their own convictions. Perhaps our children will have more luck than we do in figuring out what is important in life!

Given these significant challenges, it is no less important today that we recover a sense of what influence means in the lives of young people, and how the adults in their lives can identify and begin to exert that influence. By influence I do not mean "Doing what I say," although every parent and teacher knows that, at some point, they will have to fall back on that simple formula. Rather, it has to do with the manner in which a young person takes in the voice and example of an important adult, and makes that internal voice a formative factor in his or her life. Influence is what remains within when the parent is no longer around, the teacher is no longer at the front of the classroom, the role model has been left behind. What that young person holds on to, and uses to make sense out of life, is what I mean by the elusive but critical notion of influence.

In hoping to recover and reclaim the importance of influence, I think of four elements in the nature of adult influence that are crucial to the formation of young people.

(1) Influence is about separateness
as well as togetherness.

The reason that influence is, by its nature, so different from being constantly in touch with our children is that we recognize and value what separates us. Positive and lasting influence necessitates boundaries, including that most important boundary of all—the realization that my children, my students, are not an extension of me but are different and distinctive persons in their own right.

Many parents and teachers today pride themselves on what is commonly referred to as "being close" to their children or students. I remember one parent telling me that the moment her daughter has a question, she is on the phone to her. This, according to the mother, was a sign of the intensity of their mother-daughter relationship. When I asked her if there might be value in her daughter experiencing some time alone with a problem and figuring out some angles on her own, she looked at me as if I were speaking a foreign language.

Any parent who claims to be "close" to a son or daughter will certainly elicit the envy of other parents, including those who are getting the silent treatment from their offspring, or worry about the lack of "quality" time with their children. Likewise, the teacher in a school who is privileged to have students sharing their confidences is often looked upon with similar envy by faculty colleagues, not only for the information she may have but also the fact that she is trusted by those students. In a world that caters to the tastes of the youth, let alone prizes their attention, loyalty, consumer dollars, and sex appeal, to be in a situation of closeness with youth is to possess a great deal of prestige.

Influence, however, is not synonymous with closeness. Fortunate are those young people who have parents with whom they feel they can communicate or who have accessible role models, but adults who have positive and lasting influence on a young person are not people who are giving off signals that they need the young for affirmation and identity. Parents who push too hard for their sons or daughters to accomplish certain things in their lives are not dealing with the children in their own right. In turn, when the needs of the parents or teachers spill over in relationships with the young, they do not go unnoticed by the child or student. One of the most frequent concerns that students have brought to me over the years is that a parent at home is sharing personal problems with the child. This tempting but dangerous activity on the part of the parent helps to make the young person uncomfortable on a number of levels. The child knows that she cannot solve these problems; how come mom or dad is sharing these things with *me*? Nothing is as sobering as the sense I have from conversations with young people in these situations that they wish at some level that mom or dad would grow up.

As young people begin to incorporate influential adults into their lives, they need a space around themselves—I would call it a garden, where the ground can be fertilized and seeded. If the adult comes trespassing into that garden, nothing in the soil can really take root and flourish. There is simply no room. Adults who are mindful of the delicate but essential distance needed between young and old do indeed risk not knowing everything, not being there every time they are needed, not able to boast of that cherished notion of closeness, but they are allowing the garden to grow. They are bestowing the gift of room to their children.

---

(2) Influence is about presence.

For those who parent, teach, or guide children, the days of having all the right answers for the complex questions we encounter in the process of helping young people grow up are gone. Parenting and teaching have become infinitely more complex and multilayered activities as we watch our children "growing up in an unsteady and confusing world."[10] The old boundaries between what an adult knew and what the young did not know are also gone. Moreover, while many parents feel that it is their duty as parents to "be on top of" all aspects of their child's life, that is no longer possible. Childhood and the accompanying hazards of growing up are not something that a parent can "manage"—not only is it in the nature of children to have parts of their world cordoned off from parents or teachers, but their world is ever changing in focus and understanding. Thus the images we hold on to as we undertake the task of raising young people must give way to some other mode of authority, some other image of being in the midst of the frequent chaos and uncertainty. The notion of *presence* can appear elusive and ambiguous, but one thing it clearly is *not* is managing our children and the issues they face in life. Indeed, it is closer to the true notion of "being there" for our children than we may realize.

Presence is about standing in the midst of chaos and uncertainty, grasping whatever sense of confidence we have in ourselves, and drawing upon whatever internal resources we can in order to make a difference. As one writer defined it, "Presence is the meeting place between the inner life of a person and the outer life of action in the world."[11] It has less to do with how we respond or react to a situation than how we handle ourselves in those situations. We may feel without recourse as our child feels hurt; we may be tempted to exhort our son, daughter, or student to pursue a path or undertake an interest similar to our own. Our feelings of identification with our children are positive, but what we do with those feelings says a lot about the notion of presence.

For presence is about resisting the temptation to "swoop in" in order to solve the problem at hand, and instead living with that problem. It is to suspend hovering operations (as is the common activity attributed to what is currently known as "helicopter parenting"), and land on the ground, that place that is the source of our strength and authenticity. It can be exerting an influence through simply showing up, drawing upon our internal resources, and seeking a clearer understanding of the situation. We may have little more at our disposal than the inner conviction that it matters that we are there. It has less to do with the answers we claim to have in that situation than the fact that we have given it our fullest time and attention.

In hovering over our children, I think we have confused the valid notion of "being there" for our children with the need to act *for* our children as they encounter the tough times in life. Simply being there involves attending closely to the situation without necessarily having the power to change it. In fact, we are curiously *powerless* in situations where we are simply present.

An extreme example may shed more light on this. On an airplane flight some years ago, I was sitting behind a family whose members took up the entire row in front of me. The daughter, who was on one aisle seat, was struggling with some problem in her math homework while her mother, who sat across the aisle from her, was watching her carefully. Soon enough the sight of her daughter struggling was simply too much for mom: reaching across the aisle, she took the math textbook into her hands and said, "Here, honey, let me give it a try." Daughter put up no resistance; I suspect she was quite grateful for the help or at least used to her mother swooping in to rectify the situation.

On many occasions I have simply relied upon showing up and being attentive to the situation at hand to calm down a room of restless young people, knowing full well that they could, if they wished, decide as a group to defy me. All I had was the influence I could exert; in terms of numbers, sheer strength, and collective momentum, I was fighting a losing battle. Bringing order to a chaotic classroom quite often has to do with the degree of presence we can muster—how we remain calm and centered, undeterred or unshaken—as opposed to the use of power by raising our voice or threatening consequences.

As attractive as the notion of presence might sound, it is an immensely difficult thing to rely on or incorporate on a regular basis. It demands of us a certain amount of routine time—simply being with our children or students, and not just in the moments of crisis. If our children and students are going to be able to "soak in" our presence as adults, then they need to see a lot of us—beyond what we refer to as "quality time." Likewise, being present assumes a certain degree of focus, of "being present" or "being in the moment," and that is a rare commodity in our world of multitasking and distraction. Young people can certainly relate to the many things that pull at us and carry us away as we seek to be attentive to them—that is a factor in their own lives, too—but distractedness is not what the young person needs from us at that particular moment.

---

(3) Influence is about sitting with a problem
and not solving it.

It is a very common scenario. A parent will phone me or come to my office angry about an incident reported by his child. According to his child, a teacher or coach was unfair, had said something derogatory, had given a test that did not reflect the material that had been studied, or, in some fashion, "had it in for my child." Whether it was said in a conversation at home the night before or in a telephone call from school immediately after the incident, the parent responds quickly and decisively, taking the issue to the authorities and demanding a response.

It is a situation that my colleagues in the world of education across the country have encountered with some frequency. What the child has reported to the parent is taken literally, and the parent has already decided how the situation should be addressed. The parent comes in to see me armed with conclusions and demands for actions, without even knowing the full extent of the situation, let alone the other side of the story. Combine this tendency to be an advocate for our children with the inherent suspicion many adults today have of institutions such as schools, and suddenly the school and everyone connected with it are under indictment.

But just as we exert influence by standing calmly in the midst of a situation, equipped or ill-equipped as we may, be, so influence is also about sitting with a problem and not jumping to a premature conclusion or quick action. It is, as Robert Evans put it, "attending to the child and engaging actively, but as a listener and explorer first and only then, if necessary, as a fixer."[12] We listen to the child, we listen to our own feelings as the child's story is told ("How am I reacting to all of this news?"), and we listen for clues to the likely fact that the story is far more complex than initially reported by the child.

However, many parents feel that it is their duty, not to mention a source of pride, to respond proactively as an advocate for their child. As many parents are problem solvers in their work, so they view their role as parent, in part, as the problem solver. Parents also want very much to believe their children, hence the frequently heard retort, "My child would never lie to me," when a situation of conflict emerges. Yet, as I have encountered so many of these situations, I am convinced that the immediate move to action and blame does the child in question no good. Nor, in fact, does it serve to create the right kind of influence of parent on child.

That is because children all too frequently have but a partial view of a situation. As with all of us, the truth can be distorted in their eyes in order to suit the situation at hand or to save face. Frequently, it takes time for young people to work through a situation they find uncomfortable or seemingly unfair, and a quick reaction from parents has the effect of cutting off that needed time. What's more, often what children need from their parents is not a reaction but an attentive ear, not to mention the benefit of their follow-up questions about the nature of the incident or how the child understands it. Children would benefit far more from the time we spend asking questions, at this juncture, than our rush to take sides. "Was the coach really unfair?" we might ask. "Do you really think the teacher does not like you?" "Do you think you might have misinterpreted what that person said in the heat of the moment?" In the context of school, where so many situations can be perceived by a young person as unfair, the teacher can exert an important presence less by defending the rules of the game than probing more deeply into the example of unfairness that the student brings to the teacher.

Rather than jump to blame or indignation over what has apparently transpired, it helps the child much more to suggest alternative ways of perceiving what has occurred, what the adult in question may have intended by the comment or action, so that the child begins to understand some all-important realities in life: two people can have very different views of the same situation, and people can find themselves on opposing sides of a conflict yet still mean well and even want the best for the other. It also allows the child to begin to develop internal questions that will help him in future conflicts or disappointments when parents, teachers, and mentors are no longer around.

It is part of living in our culture to have a myriad of problems coming our way, all of which demand an urgent response. Influence is about filtering through some of those urgencies, and taking the time to probe beneath the surface of what the child reports. As one parent told me recently, "I have discovered that my child has an infinite capacity to see things from a very limited perspective." We exert lasting influence on a child when we take the time to find out more about a situation, test out alternatives, and let the child sleep on the matter for at least a couple of nights. Frequently, time allows a different perception of the situation to emerge, and the parent has embodied a far more lasting and important response for the welfare of the young person: rather than jump to conclusions, one sits with the problem.

In managerial theory, this is akin to what might be called "sitting at the bottom of the U." Once a problem has emerged, the "U" is that place where time is spent taking in the fullness of the situation and its possible responses rather than rushing to premature answers or clarity. One must listen, be creative, and do a great deal of sensing at the bottom of that "U"; we must sit with the problem if our response is to be lasting and appropriate.[13]

---

(4) Influence is about the inner voice.

Ask a number of adults what they remember most about their parents, and chances are they will eventually get around to what their mothers and fathers said to them, over and over, during the course of growing up. Frequently it was those repeated phrases that encapsulated some way of making sense of the world or expressing their deepest convictions. They might have been words of encouragement—"Always try to do your best, regardless of how you are judged"—or consoling and reassuring observations about the chance and flux of life—"Life is not always fair" or "You never know what the other person is going through." These memories would probably include stories told on important occasions in the life of the family, be it at a dinner table, family reunion or ritual, or annual celebration. Similarly, when adults are asked what they most miss about their parents, frequently they will speak of a parent's "voice," be it the actual physical voice or the manner in which that parent addressed matters that came before the family, whether serious or comical.

All of these elements make up the "inner voice" of the adult, a crucial component of what being an adult is all about. "It's up to you," a coach would say to our basketball team, over and over, in middle school. He was telling us to take responsibility for what we did on the basketball court, rather than to expect others to conform to our hopes and expectations. That voice, its calm tone, its repetition, it seriousness balanced with his unique sense of humor, has helped shape my view of life's challenges, and how I, in the long run, must take responsibility for those challenges. It comes to my aid more often than my coach would ever imagine. It is how he remains alive in me today.

The voice of which I speak is that curious compendium of convictions, phrases, stories, and tone that become a part of who we are as adults and come to our aid in moments when we must draw upon all that we have inside of us to meet the challenge in front of us. It may be the voice of a parent, the attention of a teacher, the presence of individuals who, on a regular basis or at pivotal times in our lives, were an "inspiration" to us. It is also how we incorporate those we are closest to—spouses, close friends, parents, offspring. At certain points in life we find ourselves repeating the same things they said, hearkening back to their efforts to make sense of confusing things. If someone has had a lasting influence on us, then in some fashion we have "taken them in," made them our own, folded them into our view of the world, and allowed them to shape our convictions.

In his important book *Aging Well,* psychiatrist George Vaillant continues his pursuit of those involved in the landmark study of human development begun five decades ago by the Harvard Medical School. This study has followed the health and happiness of hundreds of Harvard graduates as they pursued their careers, forged relationships, and came to terms with the shape of their lives. Now that most of them have reached their senior years, Vaillant examines how those elders have turned out—specifically, what distinguishes those who live out their seventies and eighties with a sense of completion and integrity. One of the telling features of individuals who are entering upon these decades with energy and vitality is their capacity to "take people inside." By this, Vaillant means how individuals become lively and integrated adults through their capacity to love and to incorporate internally another person into their inner lives. As Vaillant puts it: "In short, with the passage of time adolescent jerks can evolve into paragons of maturity. Such maturation, however, requires emotional development, years of experience, and a seemingly miraculous capacity to internalize others."[14]

The inner voice, it turns out, not only speaks but also shapes and defines our lives. It has much to do with the depth and scope of the lives we lead as adults. It is something we fall back on when times are tough. Even more importantly, it can be a determinative factor in how we approach different eras in our lives and whether those eras have meaning and hope for us. When Hillary Clinton, following upon her primary victory in New Hampshire, told her admiring followers that she had "found her voice" in the closing days of the primary campaign there, she received an enthusiastic and empathic response; in some way her followers knew something of what she described. To find and express that voice is viewed in our culture as a desirable and transformative destination in one's life. Yet, as a culture we have become increasingly reluctant to trust our internal voices. Perhaps we have become so reliant on the "experts"—be they in the psychological, spiritual, or child raising realms—that we place less trust in that inner voice and we do not seem to rely on our own judgment as much as we might have in a previous era.

A young, inexperienced teacher reported with surprise how she had received many telephone calls or emails, during her rookie year as a teacher, from parents of her students asking for her advice about some aspect of childrearing. "Why are they asking *me*?" she asked in a faculty meeting where we were discussing the changing role of teachers today. "I am younger than they are, and I have no kids. How did I end up giving parents advice on how to raise their kids?" Other faculty in the meeting nodded in appreciation and understanding: many of them had had similar experiences, regardless of age or experience. To tell a parent, as I have often done, "Just rely on your own good judgment," is frequently to encounter a puzzled or tentative look. We do not know whether, or how, to trust that judgment, wondering if somehow it is not in synch with what the literature on the subject might be saying.

So how do we draw upon that inner voice, particularly in an era where that inner voice goes unheard or undeveloped? Where do we find the courage to trust our inner judgment? Some people are more comfortable with delving into their inner lives than others. But we all have memories of people we admired in our past, and we can still feel resentment toward those who harmed us or sold us short. All of us have aspirations of how we want the children under our care to develop and what we want them to become. If we allow those memories to surface and those hopes to be articulated, we have the beginnings of a sense of our inner voice as well as a better reliance upon our own judgment.

Often when I meet people and tell them what I do for a living, I hear vivid accounts of the memories these people have of their own growing up years. School comes to their minds very quickly, and it does not take long for these grown-ups to plunge into their recollections of the practices and traditions that were part of their years at school. Pivotal figures, be they positive or negative, quickly and poignantly return, vivid and powerful, as if those adults were still alive today. Almost always the people they admired had a combination of high standards and some type of soft spot for the struggles of growing up that touched their souls and inspired them to do better. Those who were less admired are usually remembered as discounting or belittling others, as not being able to recognize the growing, developing young person in front of them. In almost all cases, the adults most admired demonstrated a high degree of integrity that seemed to be missing from those who are remembered in less than glowing terms.

Family memories can return just as quickly. In *Common Fire,* an important study of young people who had shown in their early personal and professional lives unusual levels of commitment to the common good, family memories were continually cited as a source of the courage, motivation, and imagination required to help meet the needs of their communities. Family moments, whether one-on-one encounters or gatherings around the dinner table, had a lasting impact and influence. Aspects of what the authors of this study called "family lore"— recounting stories and struggles going back several generations—were also significant influences on these young people. Parents and grandparents who practiced what they preached were another source of wisdom, helping to build up the internal spirit needed for the life of action in the world. As one participant, a physician in a city hospital who used to go in and out of Washington, D.C., with her mother, traveling through poor parts of the city as well as wealthy parts, recalled: "When we drove through poor neighborhoods, she talked a lot about our responsibility to do something about that. Her response was to pray for the people there. My response was to go into medicine and try to do something about it."[15]

All it takes to renew our acquaintance with our inner voices is some time to recall, to retell the stories of our significant moments growing up. In that gift of time, we bring back to life those experiences that shaped us, for good or ill, seeking to replicate in some way the elements of the positive and to learn from the negative on how *not* to live, speak, or instruct those young people in our charge. Rather than speaking of what we think we should be doing, or worrying over what we cannot do, we focus on what can equip us for what must be done as we guide our children and students.

We should also ask ourselves, "What do we most want our children to be? How do we want them to turn out as human beings?" Quite often, the answers to those questions have less to do with what they end up *doing* as with what they end up *being*. The conversation moves quite quickly from context to character. This is no surprise, as this type of question takes our view of children and students to a whole new level. I have found that when, in conversations with parents who were upset or on the offensive because of something to do with the school, I stepped back and asked them what they really wanted for their children, the tone of the conversation would change dramatically. There is the potential for common ground in such questions, shared between parents, between teachers, between parents and schools.

At the same time, we need to ask ourselves, "What are my children or students hearing from me, over and over? What type of actions are they seeing me take? What will they remember best from what I have done and said?" Humbling as it can be, we will probably discover that they are not hearing enough of what is most important to us. And we can be fairly certain that they hunger to know it.

For a variety of reasons, we adults tend to skim over and minimize opportunities to share with our children or students what gives our lives meaning.[16]

Young people need not the voice of the expert, but the inner voice of their parents and teachers. Whether that voice is ordinary or unique, liberal or conservative, strict or lenient, experienced or inexperienced, children need the sense of confirmation that comes only with the authority of the inner voice of those they most love and trust. Without the benefit of wisdom exchanged on the park bench, the regular presence of extended family, civic organizations, and places of worship, we adults feel less secure in the conclusions and convictions we hold. As much as we might be in touch with the outside world, we feel peculiarly out of touch with our inner voices. But what young people need is the wisdom and judgment shaped by the lives we lead. That is the influence they most crave.

We share this inner voice for two reasons. First, our children want and need it. Second and more important, the quality of their own lives will be shaped by the degree to which they can hear our voices and put them to use in their own lives. Our voices help to ensure that the next generation will be capable of drawing upon and speaking from their own internal voices, shaped by the convictions we hold and the miraculous capacity we all have to bring people inside of us. If we think about what we truly want for our children and students, it will be the capacity to draw upon our encouraging words and practices in those times that most test their souls and not to feel alone. But how will they develop those inner strengths and convictions if they have not first heard them from us?

We, the grown-ups, will not be left untouched or unchanged in this process. Through redrawing boundaries, developing a sense of presence, sitting with problems rather than immediately reacting to them, and learning to trust the internal voice—both within ourselves as well as within our children and students—we adults can once again exert the influence they need. In the process we may be surprised by the very different selves we see emerging within us, and we might find ourselves communicating in different and deeper ways with the young than we might have expected. It is to those dimensions of influence—difference and communication—that we now turn.

three

IS FIFTY THE NEW THIRTY?

Offering a Compelling Alternative

For a student to be educated, she has to face brilliant antagonists. She has to encounter thinkers who see the world in different terms than she does.

—*Mark Edmundson,*
The Chronicle of Higher Education
(March 14, 2008)

We must remind, cajole, and counsel ourselves, both as parents and teachers, to refrain from using children as ends for ourselves. As adults this is, I think, our fatal sin.

—*Vance Wilson,*
Headmaster of St. Albans School,
in a letter to parents (April 2008)

ON THE MORNING of September 11, 2001, news began to reach students at Trinity College regarding the events in New York and Washington. In response, many of them gathered on the main quad to share the news and resulting shock, to draw support from each other, and perhaps await some efforts at bringing the community together. Then one student leader went directly to the office of the Vice President for Student Life and announced to her, "We need adults down there on the quad."[17] The need she articulated is one that is not only essential in emergencies, but throughout the process of growing and developing as a young person: adults are needed down there, interacting with young people and helping them to make sense of this complex and confusing world.

Yet this is a message adults often do not hear. On the one hand, there is the tremendous and—from what we know of the developmental needs of young people—predictable search for adult presence. At the same time, our culture is genuinely reluctant to make any statements about what it means to be an adult today. Consider, for example, an article that recently appeared in *The New York Times* on the changing image of male models in the fashion world. It spoke of the downward direction of preference in male fashion images, moving toward ever younger and more vulnerable models of manhood. "In terms of image, the current preference is for beauty that is not fully evolved," observed one fashion publicist. "People are afraid to look over twenty-one or make any statement of what it means to be an adult."[18] Or as one birthday card quips, "If 50 is the new 30, 30 must be the new 10."[19]

Similarly, studies of young people entering into the adult world of work and responsibility tend to find it difficult to come up with apt descriptions or images of what it means to be an adult. What does the term "adult" imply for those soon-to-be or currently entering that phase of life? Rather than seeing it as a stage that is challenging, exciting, or appealing, their images of adulthood seem more foreboding.

Whether it be settling down, having a career, assuming responsibility for spouse and children, or paying the bills, most of their mental pictures connote a certain unattractive seriousness, seemingly at odds with the lightness, tentativeness, and carefree notions we associate with youth. Little wonder, then, that we elders are afraid to make statements about adulthood.

Living in New York City, I often have conversations with former students from college or high school who have moved to the city and begun living on their own, and are now engaged in their first jobs here. Often I ask them if the changes they have experienced in their lives make them in any way feel "more adult." Frequently that question is met with a look of puzzlement: "What does being an adult mean?" asked one of them in response. Rarely have I encountered a sense of pride in making at least a small step into that world; there is simply too much *gravitas* in our culture attached to whatever we might mean by adulthood. For these young people life has certainly changed, and some necessary adjustments have been made, but whether that can be identified as a move toward adulthood is another matter.

No description of adulthood is likely to cause more discomfort from adults of any age than "being different." Be it possessing different values, different tastes, or different styles—not to mention dwelling in a more serious world—that gap is not looked upon with much degree of pride or distinction. Ours is a world that seeks to minimize the differences, not highlight or revel in them. Perhaps it is our culture's worship of youthful energy and physique, or it might be that Baby Boomer residual distrust of anyone over the age of thirty (even though Boomers left that category long ago!). We are reluctant to picture adulthood as in any way a contrast to (and therefore potentially out of touch with) a culture that gears its sales pitch to the young.

Hence adults in their thirties or forties dress like young people, with less differentiation between mothers and daughters, fathers and sons. Parents often hope or claim to be as sexually free and able to delight in the same types of music and leisure activities as their sons or daughters. When parents are present in school chapel for a special event, it is often the case that the behavior of parents is more out of control than that of their children. The current adult propensity to be "rowdy," once a term we would use to describe kids of ten or twelve, is sometimes greater than that of their children. As the head of a school in the south recently told a group of parents as she attempted to bring order for a post-dinner program, "Y'all are more difficult to quiet down than your children!" Moreover, to be—as many parents like to describe their relationship with their chil-dren—"close to them," they seem to feel that similarity in style, taste, and language is a requirement. In other words, adults must descend to the level of the young in order to reach the young. To be in constant touch with one's child requires, in the minds of a great many adults, that one must be in certain key ways indistinguishable from them. We must not only know their language and preferences, we must also in some sense embody them. Little wonder, then, that we harbor a reluctance to delve any deeper into the notions of adulthood.

Technology has also contributed to a certain vagueness, perhaps even embarrassment, over the notion of being an adult. All we need to do is sit down at a computer and find ourselves in a quandary over how to do even the simplest thing. Chances are that a son or daughter—in some cases regardless of age—or student in one of our classes can solve the problem, apparently knowing the mysteries of the technological world in a way older folks simply do not. Many adults today are "immigrants" to the technological world, to use a common image, as opposed to young peo-ple who are "indigenous people" to technology, leaving adults with a sense of perpetual inadequacy when it comes to absorbing all of the advances and advantages known to the young. Compare these realities with years gone by, where we adults were the ones who had the knowledge and wisdom to impart to the young: today, technology has turned the tables, as very few of us in the adult realm have the same technical skills and adeptness as our children. They are the ones who have the knowledge to transmit; they seem to hold the keys to the future, thus leaving the adult world without one of its traditional and hallowed badges of honor.

In many of the schools I work with across the country, it is the young people who are leading the way in prodding and motivating their parents—and, in some cases, their teachers—to do more in the community, to be more conscious of the need to be good stewards of the environment, and to be conscious of the food one is eating. I talked recently to a former independent school chaplain who, together with the science and service learning faculty, taught a collaborative course in environmental ethics to sixth graders. She told me that frequently, after students had been in her class for a number of weeks, parents would come to her and explain how their children's prodding was forcing them—sometimes reluctantly—to adjust their style of living. Their influence on us is great and powerful, and in a variety of new and exciting ways we are learning more and more from our children and students. Good teachers and parents are always good learners, and the child as unofficial teacher may well be contributing to our uncertainty about what it means to be on the other side of the generation gap.

Moreover, as James Fowler has pointed out, the developing nature of our society into a pluralistic, highly mobile, self-expressive, and increasingly secular community has led to what he refers to as "our present state of ferment regarding norms for worthy adulthood."[20] Whether it is the wise parent to whom a young person comes for advice and perspective or the mentor who has something to teach to the apprentice (a role that was traditionally viewed as more than teaching mere technique), our culture does not hold up or support images of adults who are secure in their understanding of the world. No wonder, then, that we older folks, seeking to be "in touch," gravitate toward the stimulating and vivid images of youth that pervade our media. Even in all of young people's vulnerability in a time of tremendous transition, the place of the young in the world (or at least the media's portrayal of the world) feels more certain.

The results are sobering—not only for those who are, at least on paper, adults, but also for those who need to be guided by them. First of all, we have many adults today seeking to look and act as if they are younger than they really are. Second, many rely on their children for friendship and, in some cases, stability. "My son is my best friend," is a refrain I have heard far too often from parents. Third, and perhaps most tragically, this reluctance to assume the mantle of adulthood results in young people being deprived of something so essential to their overall development: the opportunity to view and learn from *difference,* the simple but singular difference between the world of the young and the world of the adult.

This last truth may be not only the most tragic but also the most difficult truth for all of us to understand. Our assumption may well be that young people learn best when knowledge, values, or whatever they may need to "get" about the world is packaged in ways that are familiar, readily accessible, and easily recognizable. As one college professor has recently written, many academics, initially befuddled by the tentative and ever-changing world of their students, choose to reach them in ways that students know well and are part of their daily life. As he puts it, "How exactly do we professors reach this kind of student? . . . Many of my colleagues have a ready answer, and the essence is this: If you can't lick 'em, join 'em."[21] The growing assumption is that students learn best when something is packaged in a language or medium that they live with every day, be it the music they listen to or the movies they watch.

If it is going to "reach them," the form of that message must be alluring, not jolting, often framed in a manner that reflects just how fixated our culture is on the consumer needs of young people.

It might be called the "mirror theory" of reaching and influencing the young. That is, the best way to connect, teach, and guide is to heighten the degree of similarity that can be found between adult and youth—bridge the gap, obviate the differences in an effort to make the connection and get the grown-up's point across. Perhaps this theory has its roots in our desire to overcome some of the conflicts experienced when adults my age were growing up in the rapidly changing world of the 1960s and 70s. Furthermore, the intense media focus on youth has made their world far more appealing. The unintended consequence, however, is that adulthood becomes more murky and certainly less appealing, both from the standpoint of the youth looking at adulthood and the adults experiencing it themselves.

I question, however, if that is the way we human beings do our best learning in life, not to mention truly understand what it means to be a responsible grown-up in this world. Diversity and difference, as we have come to know them as operative words and core values in our contemporary culture, have been largely based on racial, ethnic, and preferential differences. At the same time, they are also important when it comes to teaching, While it is always comforting to see a reflection of ourselves in what we learn and absorb throughout life, chances are that our most important and formative learning experiences have come when we find ourselves face to face with difference. In order to deal with an increasingly complex world and navigate what it means to be an adult in that world, we need something more than mirror reflections of ourselves. We need different lights, a sense of contrast—a way out, if you will, of the conflicts and cul-de-sacs of youth, even if this contrast might appear initially puzzling, unattractive, or even jolting to young people.

During one of the years I served as a college chaplain, our campus was rocked by an appalling racial incident. Feces had been smeared on the dormitory door of a student of color, and racial slurs had been written on that same door. The entire campus community—students, faculty, and administration—was appalled, not to mention very eager to identify and discipline the culprits. Even though the office of the Dean of Students was compelled to carry through on a cautious and thorough investigation of what had taken place, the community grew increasingly impatient and angry. Many could not believe such a thing could take place on a college campus where reason, tolerance, and assumed enlightenment prevailed.

As students gathered one early evening, in an open forum on the patio of the student center, they shared compelling and heart-wrenching accounts of previous incidents of intolerance on campus. Clearly, the most recent incident was not an isolated one, and students and faculty alike searched for answers to a problem that should not be surfacing, of all places, among educated people. One student of color approached the microphone and offered a suggestion that seemed surprising, to say the least, to the adults gathered there. "I think it is time," the student contended, "that our professors move into the dormitories. We need adults present there, if these problems are ever going to go away."

Many of the students gathered there nodded in agreement; few of the professors and staff were nodding, however. The proposal seemed to be a great reversal of the decades-long collegiate retreat from *in loco parentis*. As I said to a colleague standing by me at the gathering, "I guess we have come full circle!" While the proposal, not surprisingly, never gained much in the way of momentum, the cry for an adult presence, the clearly expressed need for a different tone in the dormitory, stuck with me. To find their way out of the quagmires of youth, young people need a different path, a different mirror held up to them.

In his book *Becoming Ourselves in the Company of Others: The Work of a Gay College Chaplain*, Gary Comstock, a former Protestant chaplain at Wesleyan University, reflects on this very point. As a middle-aged gay man, he expected that the bulk of his work with students would be with those who shared his sexual orientation. However, he was surprised to find that he actually did more work with straight students, even though he was clearly "out" on campus as a gay man and minister. Rather than become a primary role model on campus for gay students (as he anticipated would be the case), Comstock found that he had become much more so for straight students. "This development," he writes,

> has let me better understand what makes a good role model for students—and it is not necessarily someone who matches their experience and identity. . . . I think students are often attracted to adults who are different from themselves, who bring out their individuality rather than provide a model for it. The differences we have with students may be our best resource for relating to and helping them.[22]

Comstock is speaking of something much larger here than student ministry; he is in fact telling us something vitally important about how we learn and grow as human beings. The encounter with difference is among the best ways we internalize ideas and images. Against the backdrop of people or situations that do not mirror our own experience, we actually develop a clearer picture of ourselves and what we want out of life, of what is appealing and accessible to us. Ask any college student about her most important learning experience, and the likely answer will have something to do with encountering difference, be it a semester abroad, a community service program that connected her with a different culture, a professor who taught and made interesting a subject that had previously held no appeal, or the experience of a roommate from a very different background. "Mirroring" was not the means of growth; difference was.

As an Episcopal priest who has worked in independent schools for many years, as well as served on a college campus, I have been struck by the degree to which some of my best relationships were with non-Christian students. Those students—many of them Jewish—were not drawn to me because of their eagerness to be less Jewish. Occasionally, I have discovered, the differences could have worked even more to our mutual advantage, had we talked more about them. As one of my students in college once remarked, "I took your course because I wanted to learn what someone entirely different from me thought." He did not desire to be any less Jewish; he simply knew that one of the best ways to learn about the world was to go beyond himself and his background. So, too, we adults grow as a result of working with young people whose lives and commitments stand in contrast to our own. As Comstock concludes, "Our differences with students may be a resource that allows us to listen to them more carefully."[23] In interacting with those who are in some way different from us, we are better able to listen to ourselves, to discern what we want out of life, and to see how to approach the challenges ahead of us. In the same way, by being with grown-ups who are different from them, young people are better able to approach the adult world.

To help our children and our students best, we adults have some hard work to do. We need to figure out what separates us from young people and what makes us distinctive from them. We need to learn how the adult world, if lived in all of its fullness and promise and fully embraced, will let us be of genuine help to young people who "need the adults down there." We must figure out what are the true virtues of adulthood, what simultaneously sets us apart from the young but also, paradoxically, helps us to reach and guide them. Influence, it turns out, is about possessing a set of adult characteristics, such as patience, perspective, a sense of what constitutes real success and real failure in life, an ability to see the irony in life, and even the occasional sense of being profoundly out of step with some of the values and practices of the young.

What, we might ask, would some of those virtues look like? Here are several I have found to be important to the lives of young people.

---

(1) Adults serve as what might be called "speed bumps" to young people.

Last year, I was working with an independent school faculty on the question, "What does it mean to be an adult?" As we discussed the many complicated parameters and unclear boundaries that can make the notion of adulthood so difficult—not least to the adults themselves—we began searching for some images that captured what it truly meant to be "all grown up" in our world today. One teacher came up with the image of a "speed bump," as he put it. I asked him what exactly he meant by that image. As he replied, "Like a speed bump, an adult knows how to slow things down."

Not many of us are fond of speed bumps. They are annoying to negotiate, and if we are not aware of their looming presence, they can do great damage to our automobiles. But they obviously serve an important purpose when it comes to safety: they remind us that children are nearby, that this is not a through-street, and that we need to watch carefully and reduce our automobile's speed in that area. On a deeper level, these speed bumps can serve as reminders of another reality: that often in life we need to assume a different pace, readjust our frantic schedules, and be available for the many needs that young people bring to us. While we may be likely to picture influence in terms of acceleration, the adult often serves to influence through stopping, thinking, and de-escalating the situation.

It may be a teacher who, in a classroom discussion, urges her students to exercise caution when rushing to judgment about an idea or a situation, or to avoid neat categorizations of other people. It may be a parent who, when faced with a son or daughter experiencing great stress, urges him to ease up, put less pressure on himself, and in the process allows that child to be a child. It may be pointing out to young people that others do not move at the same pace as they do, and by understanding that, they are getting a better grasp of their relationship with the larger world. Whether it is the rush to make conclusions, the rush to keep up with others, or the rush to leave childhood behind and quickly assume a "pseudo-adulthood," young people are in need of speed bumps, and adults are at their best when they offer young people the opportunity to slow things down. In doing so, adults help young people to return to themselves and consider what is truly important.

I remember well a conversation I had with a couple whose son was struggling with his work in school. His father was pressing hard for quicker results in his son's performance in school, his organizational skills, and his management of time—all high priorities for parents these days. At one moment, as the father became flushed with frustration, his wife reached over and touched his knee. "We can't rush him on all of this," she reassured him. "Some of this will come with time." Fortunately, in her role as a "speed bump," she brought calm and perspective to her husband at a time when he, not to mention their son, sorely needed it.

Serving as a "speed bump" is hardly the most glamorous of images, particularly in a culture of great rush, yet there may be no more vital thing we do. As those who are, or who are supposed to be, adults, we can provide the essential service of helping young people (and other adults) put the brakes on the pressure to rush to do and be more. As an astute teacher put it, "The first step for the professor is to slow things down."[24] So, too, the first step in our manic culture for any adult who is intentionally or unintentionally influencing young people is to slow things down. Plenty will come with time.

---

(2) Adults serve as deep sea divers.

On a regular basis, as they plunge, explore, and ultimately develop a capacity to see beneath the surface, deep sea divers are skilled in knowing that what the sea shows of itself on the surface is hardly the full story. Likewise, we adults need to know that what young people tell us on the surface is not necessarily indicative of what they are seeking or even experiencing in life at the deeper levels. Adults are able to discern, on a regular basis, the distinction between what young people want and what they need, deep beneath the surface. The two, as it is not hard to imagine, are not always linked.

Plunging into the depths, however, is not an easy thing to do. Myth, metaphor, and mystery—the sources of life that so often dwell at the floor of our experience—are not dimensions of human understanding that rest well with a culture that is highly visible, indeed virtual, and prone to believing that what lies on the surface is all there is. Attention to nuance and subtlety goes sorely neglected in such a culture, and the deeper meaning of what people do and say—sometimes a meaning that can seem to contradict what is happening on the surface—is lost upon far too many of us. All the easier, then, to miss the fact that children are beings who do not always mean what they say, who see only part of the picture, who do not have the capacity for ambiguity that their elders are supposed to possess. We can assume quite easily that their world of concrete imagery, of rushing to judgment, and of immediate gratification of needs is all there is.

"Have you talked with the coach?" I asked the angry parent who had come to see me, upset by an incident reported to him by his daughter the previous evening. "No," came the tentative reply, "but that does not excuse what happened." Certainly not, if what his daughter reported that the coach told her was literally true. What had come to me was a story that the father had heard and interpreted on the surface. Sadly, there had not been any attempt on the part of the parent to distinguish what his daughter had wanted him to do (storm the school in her defense) from what she truly needed from her parents (hearing her out, encouraging her to sort out the situation for herself, getting the coach's side of the story, thinking for a few days about what had happened). To be sure, the father's response was quick, decisive, and based upon the assumption that what he had been told was literally true (as it may have been). But before conclusions could be reached, the depths needed to be probed. That, of course, takes more time, more attention, more embracing of the possibility that there is more to the story than what he had just heard from his child.

All of us suffer, in our contemporary world, from the "rush to judgment" mode of operation. So much comes our way and the expectation is high that we will respond to all of it in a decisive manner. As Margaret Wheatley observes: "As life continues speeding up ... we don't have time to be uncertain. . . . We rush from opinion to opinion, listening for those tidbits and sound bites that confirm our position. Gradually, we become more certain but less informed."[25]

Young people want quick action, clear solutions, and vindication for their actions and judgments. That is understandable, given the rapidly developing, sometimes chaotic mind and heart of the young person; chaos always seeks order and clarity—and wants it immediately. What young people need, however, may be quite different from what they are expressing at the time. It takes the discerning eyes, ears, and hearts of adults to plunge into the sea and consider what is beneath the surface. Of course we are eager to trust our children; by nature we want to believe them, and we want them to see us as responsive to their concerns. I have heard many parents explain to me, "My job is to stand up for my child." All of us feel a keen sense of duty when it comes to being trusting of and responsive to our children. A greater trust is needed than this, however. We must learn to trust that our children will grow into sound judgment, and part of that growth comes through encountering difficult experiences, with adults helping them to process these experiences rather than solving things for them. That is the best way to help them navigate the waters that can be both deep and treacherous, in the years ahead.

---

(3) Adults need to be willing
to be unpopular.

That may seem to be a forbidding and highly unappealing image to offer. Educators across the country have told me one of the greatest mistakes parents make with their children today is the deep desire they feel to be liked by them. Rather than doing whatever it takes to fulfill that desire, parents and teachers often need to insist on standing over and against the wishes and wants of young people, and to be comfortable with sticking to their own convictions. They need to be willing to seem decidedly *different,* not to say "old-fashioned." We do not do this because it is fun—standing alone is never fun—or because we are self-righteous, but because this is what young people need most of all from adults.

Recently I was in conversation with a colleague of mine who has been an immensely successful college chaplain. I asked him how he was doing, and his response was that he was suffering from "coolness fatigue." By that he meant that he spent a great amount of time and energy attempting to reach students at his college, and part of that effort was to appear to be culturally in synch with their wants and surface values. In some ways he had cultivated good relationships with many of those students, and he had certainly helped many see that the chaplaincy was not a fossil from the past (no small achievement!). However, there was a part of him that felt not only weary from all of the efforts, but was left wondering if what he had done, in his efforts to reach students at their own level, had ultimately born fruit, let alone taken his work as a college chaplain in the direction he wanted it to go.

All of us seek to be accessible and appealing to young people. Their approval and willingness to confide in us is something highly prized by a generation that had suffered the turmoil of a generation gap, growing up as many of us did with parents and teachers who did not understand us. Furthermore, as the writer Tom Wolfe once observed in a commencement address at Trinity College, the desire to be "cool" is a basic, fundamental, and powerful urge in human beings, as much for parents and teachers as for young people. But the attempt to embody "cool" is also fatiguing, principally because it can leave us at odds with our deeper convictions as to what young people need and what is of most value as we parent, mentor, or teach them. Being a drive which finds its power in external recognition, in the desire not only to "fit in" but to be noticed and admired in the eyes of others, coolness is by nature a drive that does not draw upon our internal resources, the self and soul that gives us the power of conviction and adherence to our beliefs. Little wonder it can be so fatiguing! As Anne Morrow Lindbergh concluded in her now classic book *Gift from the Sea*, the unending activity of trying to be something other than what we truly are can be among the most exhausting things in life.

Our great mistake, as adults, is to assume that what young people are looking for in us is a carbon copy of the urges, pleasures, and desires in life that are driving them. Adolescents may want that affirmation of themselves on the surface, but it is not what they truly need, and all that it takes is to notice how young people gravitate toward adults who dare to be themselves. Indeed, it has been my experience that they not only are drawn to them, they become very possessive of them. As a former headmaster used to say to me, "Great schools are full of eccentrics." Those who inspire young people the most are those who go out on a limb and risk the very things they long for and grapple with every day—the admiring approval of others, a way to fit in—and are thus able to show young people a way out of coolness and pretense. They need reflected back to them not similarity, but difference, not carbon copies of themselves but an inspiring "way out."

---

(4) Adults need to be willing
   to seem "old."

Again, this sounds highly contrary to the prevailing norms of our day, and may well touch upon one of our deepest fears about adulthood. All of us have no doubt pledged, at various points in our lives, not to be like those complaining elders and curmudgeons we knew in our youth. Far better, we might think, to err at the opposite extreme than to appear to be someone bemoaning the fate of the younger generation or rhapsodizing about an era gone by.

Dinah was a fine teacher at the school, who also served in the role of class advisor for the tenth grade. Having grown up in a liberal environment, where she saw herself (and others saw her) as very much a rebel and an intellectual, she prided herself on this self-image and being out of synch with the norms and customs of the culture around her. Dinah had turned into an accomplished and demanding teacher to whom many students were drawn because of her uniqueness, her strong adherence to high standards, her critical capacity to look at ideas and assumptions, and the very contrast she represented with the values of their homes and backgrounds.

I saw her the morning after a parents' evening, when tenth-grade parents got together to hear about the state of the school and the upcoming registration process for the next academic year. The conversation swerved some, however, during the course of the evening, and parents began to question pointedly the school's policy that their sons and daughters take no more than five academic courses each semester. As Dinah found herself defending the school's position, the anxious and angry group of parents challenged her about what they perceived as the school's rigidity in not allowing their children to add even more courses to their heavy schedules. As she reported to me the morning after, the evening had left her exhausted and very defensive. She told me, "I have never felt so old in my life as having a group of parents challenge me for being so firm!" No matter what good reasons she gave for the wisdom of limiting the number of courses students could take, parents wanted the freedom for their children to take more, and they saw her firmness as a sign of rigidity. Dinah had to draw the line with these parents, and it was both an uncomfortable and startling experience for her.

Perhaps "feeling old" is not something we adults are eager to experience even as we set limits and define ourselves as truly different from our children or students. It is decidedly an experience of being "uncool." However, the sense of weariness we feel from holding the line, from emphasizing our differences with young people, is a far more redeeming weariness than the weariness of conformity we experience when attempting to be in synch with our students. The former stems from something young people need: a stable and contrasting figure, known as an adult, from whom young people can learn a great deal. We are in a better position to influence young people in that way, difficult as it may be at times, than by attempting to mirror them. Old as we might feel, it is in the service of their moral and spiritual development—not to mention a source of insight for ourselves, a key that can help us understand what it means to be an adult in the first place.

In *Habits of the Heart*, Robert Bellah observes that it is a curious trademark of a highly individualized and isolated society that its members gravitate toward more, not less conformity.[26] If that is the case, then what we are describing in this world of adult difference is something truly outside the box. However, I believe that young people watch us most closely when we are our truest selves, not our most conforming selves. To understand that, however, we need to consider just how important the activity of watching can be for young people, and how what they see affects the influence we can bring them.

four

BEING WATCHED

Communicating Silently Across the Gap

They watch us all the time. The students, that is.
They listen to us, sometimes. They learn from all of
that watching and listening. Be quiet. Don't cheat.
Pick up. Don't lie. Be nice. Don't fight. They attend
to us more than we realize.

> —*Theodore R. and Nancy Faust Sizer,*
> The Students Are Watching

Inspiration, after all, is a metaphor for how we take
other people inside. Through our lungs, through
our guts, through our hearts.

> —*George Vaillant,*
> Aging Well

"MY DAUGHTER DOES not talk to me." Few admissions are more difficult for a parent to make, and few situations can produce the parental frustration and sense of power-lessness that a non-communicating child can. After all, we live in a world where communication is highly prized, in whatever form it might take, and most parents imagine that verbal communication is the surest sign of a strong, close relationship with their children. "Talk to me" is not only something we commonly hear from television interviewers, it is the wish all of us have to cement relationships and give us a sign that those relationships are close ones. It is just as frustrating for caring teachers who work with students who are clearly troubled or distracted but are not articu-lating what is on their mind and in their heart. "I've tried to get him to open up to me," the teacher reports, "but he just won't. I know something is wrong, I can tell from his work and his mood in class, but he won't tell me anything."

It can be a particularly hard thing to take for a parent, given the fact that other parents and children seem so "in touch," with the child being more than cooperative and in-volved in the whole process. In a recent article on what has come to be known as "Helicopter Parents"—those parents who are highly involved in the lives of their children, to the danger of controlling them well into college and the early adult years—collective studies show that it is not simply the need of parents to "hover," as the observers describe it, but that their children in turn have a great need for parental hovering. Many young people *want* their parents to be highly involved in their lives, indeed, yearn for more involvement even when parents decide to allow their sons or daughters to make their own decisions.[27] As one college administrator put it, "It is not just parents hovering. It's stu-dents wanting that hovering." In previous generations, it may have been the charismatic adult—the scout master, the magnetic high school teacher, the larger than life coach, the youth minister at church—to whom the young person was drawn. Today, much of that current pull is toward parents. So for a child not to exhibit that kind of willingness to talk, in this day and age, can seem like a cruel defeat for the parent.

It is important to remember, however, that communication can be a power tool in the hands of the young. At some level, they understand how important it is for their parents to know what is going on inside of them. To withhold that information puts the child in an immensely powerful position, perpetually frustrating the parents and making them feel inadequate. This can be particularly true in an age when the actual time spent with a child is at a minimum—and what parent would not want the little time spent together to be filled with ample and meaningful communication?

From the standpoint of a teacher, I have learned that the least likely time that a young person is prone to communicate with an adult is the one time that adult wants to sit down and have a meaningful conversation! Again, at some level, the child realizes that she holds many of the cards when Mom or Dad wants her to "open up." As open communication increasingly becomes a hallmark of good teaching, with teachers encouraging students to "come and see me if you have any problems," the student can exercise what little power he has in the student-teacher relationship by controlling the extent to which he is forthcoming and transparent.

Instead, any honest and open communication usually occurs at the child's discretion. It may come on a family trip, when parent and child are doing a task together, or—perhaps the most inconvenient time of all—when the parent is heading out the door to work. I have always been amazed at the number of times students have brought up important issues in their lives or crucial questions on their minds and hearts at those moments least amenable to a good response. How can I answer a question about the meaning of life when class is ended, everyone is headed for the door, and I have any number of tasks ahead of me back in the office? Of course, young people may not yet understand or appreciate the difference between hospitable and inhospitable times for adults to entertain their questions. Just the same, when it comes to communication, the ball is in the young person's court. We cannot force it from them or expect it of them, not to mention pull it out of them.

Admittedly, this runs contrary to our need to pack as much depth and substance into the short time we have with children—what has become known as "quality time" today. Honest and open communication demands a great deal of time to surface, and this is something very few parents or teachers have a lot of these days. It tends to surface on that unexpected occasion, particularly after a good deal of ordinary conversation has taken place, or as adult and child focus on a task or project. This allows the mind, heart, and mouth to head in a variety of directions.

Whether we are parents, teachers, clergy, or that rare but important adult who by chance befriends a young person, we cannot assume that the occasional or frequent distancing of young people means a sincere desire not to have adults in their lives. This is one important way in which taking young people literally does not help them. What young people say and mean can be very different, and being an adult in the truest and most mature sense of the word requires us to take a second look, to see beneath the surface, and to avoid becoming entangled in what the young may seem to be telling us.

Whether or not we have the time for an ample amount of verbal communication with our children or students, and whether or not those young people are talking to us, there is nonetheless some good news: talking is not the only form of communication taking place between the adult and the young person. There is, for example, what they are *hearing* from us, something that does not end when they stop speaking to us. Our young people may not be talking much, but they do not discontinue hearing us— in fact, hearing what adults have to say then is as important to them as ever. Our children and students are taking in what we have to say regardless of whether they are talking back; as one wise school head has assured her parents, "The fact that your children stop talking to you is no sign that they have stopped listening to you." In fact, it is all the more important that we keep communication open—our children and students need to know of our closeness and caring concern as much (or even more) when they have shut down verbally as when they are forthcoming. As with so many other elements of growing up, increasing independence, distance, and seeming lack of interest in what adults have to say have little to do with the degree to which young people still need that adult influence. As Robert Evans observes, "Even as adolescents turn away from parents, they also draw heavily upon them."[28] Influence demands that we never stop talking, regardless of the surface reaction we are getting from our children and students.

Yet there is an even more influential mode of communication, I would maintain, at work in the interaction between adult and child. It is as lasting and powerful as anything we say, and is a more telling symbol of the bonds we share than talk. It also happens to be one of the most overlooked forms of communication in a highly verbal age, and it is the one activity perhaps all children and young people have in common: the activity of taking things in, of *absorbing*. The act of absorbing is a means of communication far more powerful than words, far more lasting in its impact that anything we might say. It goes on silently, but in the stillness of this mode of communication the waters are running deep and are lasting.

Adults who live among or work with young people can likely recall times in which they have discovered they were being watched. It usually comes when we are least expecting it, and all too often when we most wish we ourselves were not on display. We look up and—whether it be a young child in his receptiveness or a teenager in her cynicism—we notice them studying us, taking us in, and noting our words, gestures, and moods. It is a startling and, at times, frightening experience. "What are they looking at? What are they thinking?" we ask ourselves. The reality is that this activity takes place far more often than we might imagine. The art of studying adults, noting their strong and weak points and internalizing those adults into the soul of the young person, is among the most persistent yet mysterious habits of those who stand on the threshold of the world we call adulthood.

At the high school where I served as head, we had seated lunch every day. It was something we held onto for the purpose of building community in spite of tremendous pressures to do otherwise. At the end of that lunch, we had a rather prolonged period where students made announcements, many of them quite clever and others crossing the line of appropriateness. To add a sense of *gravitas* to the occasion, I used to wander around the dining room, no doubt conveying a sense of presence and whatever amount of authority I embodied. Admittedly, I set myself up in that situation to be stared at by students as I walked past their tables. Yet it continually startled me when I would glance up and see students looking at me. Whenever an announcement had passed beyond the limits of propriety (and such announcements almost always provoked laughter, that great and precious commodity of adolescence), eyes would invariably turn toward me to see how I was reacting. Routinely, I had to ask myself, with so many eyes on me, just how I would react—with anger, with a smile on my fear, with a mysterious neutrality? Even after many years of experiencing this phenomenon, I found myself surprised by how much they studied me. We are prone to overlook and underestimate this activity of growing up, this "taking in" of adults by those who aspire to adulthood. As adults we are likely subjects of study whether we are close to those who are watching us or not.

The art of studying adults was also practiced in the classroom. Those who know me are well aware that I have a real love of shoes, and no doubt I have purchased far more shoes in my adult life than I really need. One day in my tenth-grade ethics class I was explaining a rather intricate philosophical formula, when a student in the front row raised his hand. I thought he was about to ask a question relevant to the deep and probing ideas I was explaining. After I called on him, he looked at me and, with a dead-pan face, asked, "Do you by any chance own a shoe factory?"

It happened in chapel as well, where I was also on display. Over the years I was continually surprised by their comments after chapel about my reactions to what was being said by one of our guest preachers. "You looked really bored today in chapel," one of them might report following the service, even though I thought I was doing my best to appear interested in a lackluster sermon. Similarly, even though I did not know I was showing it, students were quick to point out when I seemed to be highly engaged: "You were really grooving up there with the preacher!" I remember one student saying, even though I don't remember what made her say it.

So if I were to point to the one definition of adulthood that I feel is most apt, most compelling, it is *adults are the ones who are being watched*. We are being watched when we take liberties with the rules of the road on the highways; we are being studied when a reaction—disapproval, laughter, or a clear decision—is needed from us. We are being watched for our consistency, our nervousness, our times of worry and frustration. Perhaps we are being watched most carefully when we cry, or seek to apologize, or find ourselves in some way displaying our vulnerable or fragile ways of dealing with what the world demands of us.

Jerald was one of those students who seemed to watch me carefully during chapel services for the school. He would give me regular reviews of my sermons, or those done by others. "A little too long today, Reverend," came the critique one day. "I think you need to vary your humor at the beginning of the sermon; these Vermont stories are getting tiresome," came another. Fortunately, there were those times when he identified an "awesome sermon," and given his overall propensity to be critical of my preaching, those stood out, indeed meant something to me. At one point he told me I was on the verge of being "too stylistic" in my sermons, warning me that the substance of what I was trying to say was at risk of being lost in the flourish of the delivery of them. At first, I interpreted this as his need to find a way of being critical (criticism, as Fowler has told us, is one of the predictable, albeit, awkward ways that young people attempt to be close to their elders!). A subsequent chapel service helped me realize, however, that he was searching for something deeper: in that particular service, I lost track of what I was supposed to do next, and, as he reported to me in his "post-chapel review," this was the first time he had seen me betray uncertainty in my role as leader in the chapel service. I could see from the expression on his face that this experience came as a relief to him, as if he had made a new discovery about me. Although I did not relish the experience, I realized that for Jerald it was important. For the activity of watching adults is a comprehensive process, touching not only upon the young person's need to take in models of experience and inspiration, but also her need to encounter models of struggle and fallibility, and how those particular adults make sense of their own shortcomings in a world that will in some way, inevitably, bring them to light.

To be in contact with young people on a constant basis is to be the object of much scrutiny, and at times the burden of it can feel overwhelming. No wonder so many adults seek to shun the task of mentor or role model, for the demands upon us in such situations are enormous. Likewise, we are deeply aware of the fact that there have been many times when we were being watched and we did not realize it—we were the subject matter and simply did not notice it—and we truly wonder what those youngsters took away from the exercise. How often have they caught us out in hypocrisy, in failing to practice what we preach? We hear them often talking of adult hypocrisy, and we worry that we are in some way displaying it in our own lives. The good news, however, is that in fact young people *need* to see what they perceive to be hypocrisy in us. As James Fowler reminded us in *Stages of Faith,* it is the task of the developing young mind and heart to seek out and identify hypocrisy.[29] Such is the manner in which a young person deals with the development of internal ideals and the clashing of those ideals with the realities of the world.

For example, in *Speaking of Faith,* radio journalist Krista Tippett recalls the time when she began to recognize the hypocrisy and contradictions in the behavior of the people around her: "There was a chasm between the genuine importance of the issues at hand and the moral maturity of some of the people who were defining those issues and literally running the world.... Up close to power at a young age, I experienced a problem deeper and more basic: powerful people often had impoverished inner lives."[30] Tippett's experience is not only far from unusual, it is formative. It led her to make some important decisions in her life, including the desire never to live a life of contradictions in the manner she had observed in others. Rather than being a jarring experience, seeing hypocrisy and contradiction is something young people need to encounter, in fact are quite likely to encounter. One thing we can guarantee, from the youthful scrutiny of adults: they will search for hypocrisy, and that search will be successful!

Luckily, it is the fullness of adult life that young people need to see in us, not just us on our good days. Young people are aware, at a much earlier age than we expect, of the ambiguities and compromises that adults must make, and they hunger for guidance in the cultivation of the vast repertoire of responses that need to be developed. Their studying of us is crucial, and part of that process is acquaintance with what is eloquent and what is impoverished in our lives. Much to our dismay, we will find out that our mistakes are as worthy of contemplation and understanding as are our acts of heroism. To be reminded of this all-important activity of young people is, I believe, the first step toward grasping what we must be about in helping young people develop an inner core. It is also, I believe, the first step in understanding what I stressed in chapter three—what young people need to see reflected back to them is not a mirror image of themselves, but *difference*. It is difference, not similarity, that instructs them and leads them out of their developmental gridlocks in life. Just as we seek out conflict or tension in the novels we read or the stories we follow in the news, so what truly absorbs young people is the difference that can emerge when the world of the young and the world of the adult collide.

This does not mean, of course, that we are off the hook in our need to lead exemplary lives as adults. It is no good simply to laugh off our mistakes as adults, as if we are "only human." Those mishaps will come with the territory of living, and we will have ample time and occasion to show the vulnerable points in our lives. What young people need to see from us is a combination of the moments when we truly shine as adults—when we stand for our convictions and make decisions based on what is right as opposed to the expedient or popular—with the times we fall short of that. In our desire to appear more youthful, we adults may mistakenly back off from moments of passionate conviction or let ourselves off the hook too quickly for the times we fall short. A reminder of the fact that young people are watching us—more often than we might think—should bring us back to reality.

I once made a decision that was very unpopular with the senior class, whereupon a delegation from the student council came to see me to say how disappointed they were in my leadership and how out of touch I was with the tone and ethos of the school. I listened carefully to them, attempting not to be defensive. It was, nonetheless, a tough experience to endure, as these were the student leaders I most trusted, and to have forfeited their trust was a great letdown for me. The meeting ended with my telling them that the experience had not been an easy one for me, but that I appreciated their taking the time to let me know how they felt about it. There was an uncomfortable silence as they departed, and I left school for home that day very discouraged. That evening I got a telephone call from the president of the class, who was part of that meeting and was as vocal as anyone regarding the degree to which I was "out of touch" with the school. He called to say how impressed he was with how I listened to all that they had to say, and to thank me for the tone I took with them. Looking back, I think he saw that I was in a leadership situation he might face himself in the future. And in my response he saw an example—a far from ideal example—of how it is sometimes the case that when we are on the receiving end of criticism, one of the best options is simply to listen.

Again, we model adult behavior not because we want to look good or assure ourselves that we are doing the job we should be doing, but for the sake of the young we are bringing along in the world. To be an adult, to exercise influence, involves a reliance upon a repertoire of images and experiences that live inside of us, that come to our aid and allow us to thrive as adults. Our reactions when we are angry, when we are caught off guard, when we are the butt of criticism or are having to make a very difficult decision, are powerful moments for our children and students, for in those moments they are being offered models of how an adult can respond. If we can give them mature models to emulate, they will go a long way toward becoming the healthy adults we want them to be.

Furthermore, the examples of adult behavior they internalize when we face disappointment or setbacks are perhaps the most important models we offer them. If my conversations with educators across the country ring true, their chief concern with the students they teach and the parents they work with is that we all have a tendency, in our contemporary culture, to want to rescue our children from painful experiences. Many have written that such regular rescuing from the pain of life—even though it is terribly difficult for us to watch them endure such experiences—will render young people unable to deal with the disappointments, setbacks, and hurts that they will inevitably encounter throughout their lives. So, too, many have expressed concern about whether young people today will have adequate "coping skills" to meet those challenges. Beyond just coping skills, I would maintain that our children and students need to see how we ourselves are managing these stresses—how we make sense of, react to, and ultimately learn from the disappointments and failures we so often experience in life. If the model of the powerful adult who rescues is the only image they are able to draw upon in such times, then they will indeed be highly unprepared to take on the many sorrows and challenges that life will deal them.

In conclusion, what should we keep in mind when we are aware of the fact that our children and students are watching us and absorbing the lessons of our behavior? What are some of the guideposts that will help us when we are faced with difficulties and challenges that demand the best from us, and the studying eyes of the young are not far away? What do we, as some of the primary actors on this stage, with our young people being the audience, convey to them about how we operate in our respective roles? Here are three suggestions.

---

(1) Never fall back on "Do as I say and not as I do."

While it may rest upon a trustworthy and verifiable view of human nature—that we often fall short of our goals and ideals as human beings—we adults need to stop letting ourselves off the hook. Offering guidance and advice to children and adolescents has no merit if it is not backed up with a serious attempt to live out what we say we want them as young people to incorporate into their lives. Otherwise, one of the major reasons that adults positively influence young people—their trustworthiness and their capacity, in the words of one educator, to "live a less divided life"—is at great risk.[31]

In other words, we do need to live our lives with moral seriousness, for the way we live that life has tremendous meaning to the young who are watching us. No technique, no tips on parenting, no lesson plan will replace the value that comes from a young person being able to witness and absorb a life that takes the *how* of what we do seriously. Just as books on parenting, over the years, have made the point that a parent should never threaten a punishment that she is not prepared to deliver if it comes to that, so an adult should never preach to youth about values or commitments that she is not prepared to embrace in her own life. When a child listens to a parent or teacher go on about something that should be done in the world, indeed, something that the younger generation should be taking on, but knows that this parent or teacher has no plans to do these things himself, then he is spouting merely empty words. The exhortations become vacuous.

Perhaps it is our lack of confidence in ourselves as adults, or our hesitation to hold ourselves up as role models or rely upon our personal convictions, but parents and teachers today have one vital thing in common besides a clear interest in the well-being of the young: both tend to discount the day-to-day influence they have on young people. I see this influence at work in the deep desire most adolescents have to please their parents, perhaps the most formative and motivating force in many of their lives. I see it when a student is hurt by a passing comment from a teacher: what may have been meant to be a joke or some good-natured kidding turns out to feel like a devastating critique of his character. As often as not, that student has been working hard to impress his teacher, and the passing comment is quite hurtful. For both teacher and parent, the impact is evident in the things that children remember that we have said, indeed can recall with great clarity and immediacy, though we may have forgotten about them long ago. We adults so often sell ourselves short in this regard; we forget the lasting impact our words and actions can have.

This perhaps unintended influence may be the most grave and challenging element of adulthood, but maturity is a serious business with strong repercussions. Our actions demand careful, ongoing scrutiny, and there must be a connection between words we use and the actions we take.

---

(2) Sweat the small stuff.

One of the primary goals we have for our children is that they be happy. What our desire for their happiness can do, however, is cause us to discount or neglect things that may stand in the way of that happiness, at least in the eyes of the young person. They may also stand in the way of our living peaceably with our children. It may be a clean room, showing up at school on a regular basis, or even holding to our sense of what is best for that child (as I have heard some parents say, when confronted by the fact that their son had been drinking, "At least he is not doing drugs!"). A common form of advice to adults these days is not to get caught in the web of arguments and confrontation that comes with some of the battles we have to fight with young people. To be sure, we do need to determine what battles to fight, but some of those "smaller battles" actually are very important ones.

Since parents spend less time with their children than in the past, we also want the time we do spend together with them to be as happy and free of pain or conflict as possible. However, there is meaning to be found in dealing with the perennial issues that absorb so much of our time and energy and good will. It may seem trivial, as we balance what truly is important with what is less so, but to the young person, absorbing all she can about the contours of the adult world, focusing on small stuff—not for the sake of the smallness of it, but for the largeness of it in the long run—does have importance.

Recently I had the privilege of visiting a boarding school where many students had experienced emotional, learning, or disciplinary issues in their previous school or at home. They are being given a second chance to make progress; seeing firsthand the care of the faculty and staff at this school was truly extraordinary. During my time at the school I was given a tour of the dormitories and was struck by the neatness and order routinely expected of the students in terms of how they made their beds, how they arranged their clothing, and the degree to which they were required to keep their individual spaces clean and clutter-free.

At first I thought this expectation of order might be a bit excessive, and I suspect that there have been a number of students who simply could not live with the attention to "small stuff" demanded there. So I asked a group of them how they felt about the attention to detail and order that was so much a part of their daily lives. One of the students responded, "It can be a real pain, keeping things so clean and orderly, but I think we discover through being able to handle the smaller, routine tasks that we might be able to take on the larger tasks of life."

I was struck by the depth of his observation; he understood that smaller things need to be taken care of before we are truly able to take on some of those larger tasks of life. Obviously, the expectations of that particular school are not for every child, and part of the genius of that school's emphasis on order is to give students who may have not experienced much of a sense of accomplishment in life more of it. However, the experience reminded me that small things *do* matter in our dealing with all young people—what they say, how they treat other people even in passing, and how they show respect for themselves in the clothes they wear and the manner in which they keep their rooms. All of these things do in fact have a relationship to what we see as the bigger issues, be they happiness, success, or fulfillment in life (and note that they are not automatically related). In the midst of what may seem to be a trivial argument between parent and child or teacher and student, whether in finishing homework or walking the dog, we need to remind ourselves and perhaps put into words that what may seem trivial right now has its own place as we move through the tasks of life—a place in our children's lives as well as our own. It may well be that in the seemingly trivial, young people absorb some of their most important images of adulthood, as well as find the small successes necessary to go on to what is truly important to them.

---

(3) Offer more challenge
   and less "support."

Few words carry with them such cache and impact these days as "support." We want and expect those close to us to be "supportive"; we see our role as a teacher or parent as one where we "support" the young; the quality of any relationship is often judged by the degree to which we support someone and feel supported. Support, as an image and a concept, has become all-consuming: it is a word, I would contend, that either has lost its meaning or needs tremendous clarification as we continue to use it in the years ahead. For "support" has far-reaching implications for the unspoken activity of absorbing. A parent may think she is supporting her child by letting her off the hook with "mental health days" at home; a teacher may feel he is supporting a student by openly criticizing a decision the school has made. But it is essential to realize that *agreement* does not always mean support, and the two are in great danger of being confused in the formation of adolescents. When young people see examples of support from adults that are nothing more than siding with them, or going on the offensive for them, they are being exposed to only one of the ways we adults support them.

Moreover, we often assume that support is the same thing as advocacy, particularly a style of advocacy that takes sides and goes to another's defense. There are times when we do need to show support in this way, but not to the exclusion of challenging the youth in our care, helping them see another side of the situation, and simply listening to them without rallying to their side. If we are truly serious about supporting young people, there needs to be a mixture of different kinds of support: at times it means moral exhortation, at times holding them accountable, and at times disagreeing and offering an alternative perspective. At other times, it means a parent soothing and holding a child, or a teacher giving a student a break. Support is a complex process, aimed at helping young people deal with many and varied issues in their lives. If support only means taking sides, rushing to the child's defense, or shielding her from pain, we are limiting its scope and impact, particularly as young people take in and learn from examples of how support works. If they only see support as a teacher, parent, or boss agreeing with them, then they risk entering into the adult forays of life unequipped with images or memories of what happens when people they respect and trust do not agree with them, when they must make a lonely decision, or when they cannot rely upon a person, automatically taking them at their word.

Clearly, this pattern of young people watching us and taking us in is a process that is both daunting and highly nuanced. It demands the best in us. We have to learn the ability to live lightly with our shortcomings, to pay attention to the words we use and how those words can be so easily distorted in the eyes of a young person. It demands that we get our hands dirty with the nuts and bolts of living, if we are truly to relish the moments of happiness and joy and long-term flourishing. In other words, it demands a lot more probing and understanding than we have given it already. It is to that effort to find some credible models of adulthood that we turn next.

five

EMBRACING ADULTHOOD

Reaching Inward for Inspiration and Influence

Hayes had such a profound effect on his players that years after he died, they would often speak of him in the present tense.

—*Michael Rosenberg,*
speaking of Ohio State football coach
Woody Hayes, in War as They Knew It

To my parents:
Thank you for being the most supportive and loving people in my life. Raising a son who constantly changes his mind, his focus, and often his hairstyle, has provided many challenges and unforgettable moments. Thank you for being there for every one.

—*Graduating senior,*
St. Albans School yearbook

AS GRIM AS OUR society might make it out to be, adulthood is chock full of surprises. Imagine the surprise of discovering as life goes on that the person on the outside—with accompanying wrinkles (what William Sloane Coffin once called the "credentials of humanity") and sagging muscles—is not the person on the inside. That the person on the inside feels a lot younger than the outside wrappings may indicate. There is also the surprise of having to do something that we may have anticipated in theory but still comes as a shock: the care of our aging parents. In my travels I end up sitting in airports a great deal, privy to cell phone conversations I do not want to hear. I am struck, in these inadvertent and unwanted eavesdropping on other people talking, how often the conversation is about taking care of one or both parents, as when a brother is briefing his sister on the status of the new care facility for their mom. Nothing can jolt us into the adult world as powerfully as the reality that the tables do indeed turn, and that our parents may end up relying upon us for routine and sometimes extensive care.

Then there is the surprise of the teacher who, when talking with students about an event that seems recent to her, realizes that all of the students listening were actually born *after* the event in question. First it was Vietnam, then the Reagan era, now the Berlin Wall, and soon it will be September 11, 2001. These surprises come with dramatic impact for many of us who may not have a full understanding of what adulthood really means. We do not simply ease into adulthood on a gradual basis; some of it comes at us quite unexpectedly.

One surprising realization that came to me gradually, as I moved into my adult years, was that I am ending up to be a lot more like my parents than I would have suspected. Theoretically, I knew that is often the case: courses taken in seminary on counseling and family process referred frequently to the "sins of the fathers" being passed on to the next generation. A parish rector I admired a great deal, who was my supervisor in field education, once said that, as he advanced in age, he was finding it ironic that he was ending up more, not less, like his father. I found that hard to imagine at the time. However, the unfolding of this truth of adulthood was a startling one for me, mixing happy times with humble ones. I realized, for example, that I had a great deal of my father's shyness about expressing emotion; at the same time, I also found myself with time drawn toward my mother's more open and direct expression of feelings. I also discovered that while early on I shared many of my father's Democratic tendencies, my mother's Republican leanings gradually surfaced within me as well.

My parents were both educators in the local public school system where I was a student, and many of my parents' siblings were also teachers or school administrators. My sister also became a school teacher. Throughout my growing up years, the life of school was dominant and ever-present in our home. School was one of the prevailing topics of conversation at dinner, and I absorbed their conviction early on that teaching was not only a respectable but desirable career option to consider. My mild form of adolescent rebellion, however, was to go another route, eventually ending up in seminary and being ordained in the church. As with many young people who get ordained, the decision was a source of great surprise and puzzlement to my family, who nonetheless supported me every step of the way.

A few years following ordination, however, I was serving as chaplain in a school in New York City. One spring day I was walking back to my office following a meeting with the head of school in which I found I was to named one of his assistant headmasters. It was a moment of great pride and elation for me, yet in that trip back to my office, I suddenly stopped dead in my tracks. Although the vocational route was circuitous, I had ended up following in my father's footsteps. For the preceding few years I had been traveling a path that, unknowingly, was leading me back to the career of my father.

Since then, when I have asked a parent, for example, "How is Sarah doing in college?," I realize that I am doing the same thing as my father, who frequently reported to us at dinner his conversations with parents whose children had gone off to college. On many occasions, I could almost feel the spirit of my father asking that question for me, within me, as my years of working in schools began to unfold. Similarly, I would enter a classroom or travel down the hallway of the school, and suddenly notice that the students there had stopped talking about whatever the topic might be, for fear that I might be listening to them. Then I recalled how my father elicited a similar reaction when he would walk down the hallways as the superintendent of my school. Or a conversation about one of my student's personal life would emerge as we were working together on a community service project, and I would remember how my mother would report similar conversations as she and one of her student assistants cataloged books in the middle school library where she served.

Or it may be the parent, in a serious conversation with her daughter, who says, "What goes around comes around" and realizes it is the exact thing her mother used to say, over and over, at the dinner table; or the moment when, after hours of argument with a son, the father has to resort to the final rationale and source of authority used by his own parents: "You will do it because I *said so!*" Or it could be the teacher who uses a catchy line in her classroom, only to remember that she first heard that line from one of her own teachers. Whatever the context, there are times in this adult life when we are brought back to the familiar: as much as we may have vowed never to allow it to happen, or as often as we rolled our eyes in response to something our parents said—over and over—as we grew up, it turns out that we are a lot more like our parents or mentors than we might have imagined or desired.

Thus adulthood is, in part, about realizing just how close we are to our parents in so many of our life patterns.

As much time as we might have spent living our lives in opposition to our parents in our earlier years, we find at some point in adulthood the surprise of connection with them, in ways we may have found unthinkable in earlier years. As the years progress, we discover that our moods, our responses to situations, and our values have a lot more in common with mom or dad than we thought. In some cases it is a joyful realization; in others we are left with little recourse other than to make peace with it.

These moments of realization, be they welcome or unwelcome, do give us a clue as to the big tasks of being an adult, particularly as we consider how we can better care for the young. Simply deciding to be "more adult" is not enough: we need to draw upon our own internal resources for models of adulthood—examples of grown-ups who influenced us as we ourselves grew up, individuals whose spirit and inspiration lives on in us and can now come to our aid as we grapple with the enormities of the job of being adults for the sake of young people. We cannot do it alone, in the abstract; we need the help and the influence of those who have been part of our lives.

As I consider the models that in some way live on in me, I recall the pastor at my childhood church. His dynamism and his capacity to rouse anger and indignation in my parents, yet still elicit their deep loyalty, was working within me as a child, no doubt sowing the seeds there of a future vocation. I recall that when in moments alone I "played preacher," like many clergy-to-be do when they are young, that pastor was my model. For example, in pointing out some of the injustices done to the poor, he used the refrain "No room in the world" over and over in one of his sermons. Decades later, I can still recall those words, and other refrains I heard over and over. Those preaching memories helped me—without knowing it—make sense eventually of how the pulpit can be a place where story and metaphor can help express some of the deepest truths of our faith.

In later years I had the influence of the band director at my high school who expected great things of us yet also clearly loved being among young people. I recall with astonishment how he would not react in anger when I would, as the drum major of the band, defy him for one reason or another, but nevertheless hold his ground and stand firm in his decision. Then there were the moments when, due to my reluctance to practice, I clearly disappointed him; those moments when I was not at my best still haunt me, and often I yearn for the opportunity to live them over, proving to him what I could do. More than any other significant adult in my life, he probably saw me in my fullness—both the good and the bad—and perhaps that is why, through the years, I ended up visiting him many times in his home.

Still later, there was the Russian history professor in my sophomore year of college who astonished me one day when I received a C– on my first paper. Beside that grade on the paper there was the all-important note, "Please see me," which I, in my confusion and disbelief, did quite quickly. "It is time you learned how to write clearly," he told me in that meeting. Until that point I had coasted by with whatever natural talent I might have had as a writer and organizer of thoughts, but this professor would have none of it: "It is time you worked at your writing," he added. It was an eloquent example of how such upsetting moments of surprise and challenge can provoke turnarounds in our lives.

By intentionally drawing up from within us some of the key people who have modeled adulthood for us, we accomplish a number of things. We can gain confidence for the difficult and demanding tasks of adulthood; we can see that it can be done with the help of those adults who truly do live on within us. We realize how important life lessons were learned in the process, and how the initial experience that led to these lessons turns out to be very different in tone and importance in the long run. Through reaching back and summoning up these models, we learn a great deal about ourselves, and how we came to be the people we are today. It is a complex but fertile undertaking that can help us not only make sense of our own lives but also become better and more influential adults for the sake of the next generation.

As I remember the pivotal adults of my life, it is their balance of qualities that remains most lasting and important to me—remaining firm while being compassionate, gentle but clear in what they expected, challenging yet also eliciting loyalty, enjoying the young but not trying to be like them. In returning to those models we knew during our growing up years, we may encounter some that we would rather forget—adults who did some damage to us in the process of growing up. The teacher who could not see the good in us, the parent who withheld love, the mentor who in some way disappointed us by turning out to be, at least in our eyes, a hypocrite. However, we need to move beyond seeing those people in our lives purely as victimizers. In revisiting their negative influence, we may discover that they also inspired us to make a crucial decision never to pass on to the next generation what they passed on to us. Educator Paula Lawrence Wehmiller speaks of the way effective teachers so often emerge from bad education as well as good:

> The source of so much of the best teaching is that very same injury. Teachers who have been hurt by the hostile environment of the schools they attended as children . . . take that same hurt and turn it into the strength of their teaching. We go back to school and there we right for someone else what was wrong for us. In the process of righting it for the children we teach, we are righting it for ourselves too.[32]

Thus part of our spirit of dedication and moral conviction may in fact derive from the influence of those who injured or disappointed us, sowing the seed of a commitment to and a moral seriousness about the needs of the next generation.

At the conclusion of one of his later books, *Dimensions of a New Identity,* Erik Erikson writes that in youth "you find out what you care to do and care to be.... In young adulthood you discover whom you care to be with.... In adulthood, however, you learn to know what and whom you can take care of."[33] Many things can keep us from taking on that adult task—whether attending to our own needs or feeling we are not up to it. A helpful aid in getting us to the point of welcoming and incorporating that adult task is the return to the images of important adults whose influence lives within us, those who, when we were learning about what we care to be and who to be with, provided us with the confidence to continue. In the process they imparted to us some of the care that Erikson describes as being the cherished discovery of finding out, in adult life, "what and whom you can take care of." As with all sources of inspiration, those models never leave us; they are ready now to fuel our imaginations and help us begin to be better adults for our students and children.

WISDOM FROM INFLUENTIAL ADULTS

These images not only inspire us to move forward, they also provide us with an abundance of practical helps in terms of the manner in which we go about influencing young people. As we draw upon our own sources of inspiration, so we find there some clues as to the concrete ways we go about learning what and whom we take care of. Here is some of the practical guidance they have given me.

---

(1) Never miss an opportunity to tell
young people what they are good at.

I will never forget the moment when my tenth-grade speech and drama teacher asked to see me after class. This teacher was one of the first adults I had known, beyond my own parents, who could truly relish the work she was doing in life. In that meeting not only did she tell me how well I was doing in class, but she expressed her sense that I had a particular talent in these disciplines. She then went on to say how she hoped I might consider some type of career in speech or drama.

I never ended up on the stage or as a speech teacher (although there is plenty of drama and speaking in the vocation I ultimately chose), but that context—a teacher I admired taking me aside and pointing out a talent I had that might translate into future work—was one of the most important points in my early high school years. In fact, it helped to serve as one of the ways I was able to begin digging myself out of a depressive rut I fell into during that very year in high school. Ever since, I have loved the opportunities I have had to tell students how much I thought they would be good at something later on.

Much has been written about the way in which our contemporary society exhibits what we might call "praise inflation"—how, in an effort to raise the self-esteem of our children, we trump up their modest accomplishments into award-winning bumper stickers: "I am the proud parent of an honor roll student," and so on. Our young people have become used to affirmation and praise on a regular basis, and it will certainly have an impact on the challenges we will face in dealing with them as adults. That does not take away, however, from the deep need that young people have to know, in the words of my student in the first chapter,

"What am I good at?" By this I am referring to strategic, meaningful times when we genuinely see a way in which a young person is giving us a telling clue to the possible endeavors—be they vocational or otherwise—to which she might be aspiring in life. Those poignant moments when we take a young person aside and let him know, from our perspective, of an important skill we see developing, is one way adults can provide the all-important link between who the young person is now and what he or she will become as an adult.

One of the things I most enjoyed about working on a college campus was the opportunity to tell students I thought they would be very good at ministry or teaching. At first such a suggestion sometimes came as a shock (imagine being asked by the college chaplain, "Have you ever thought about going to seminary?"!), but almost always that was followed by some recognition of where it might come from, or perhaps the hopeful reply, "Gee, I never thought about that." Whether or not those students in any way followed that suggested path is purely secondary to the confirmation they received when, totally out of the blue, they were recognized—not with awards or inflated praise—by an adult for having some type of long-range capacity to give back to the world.

(2) Help them to separate the essential from the non-essential.

Astute adults undertake, on a regular basis, a process of sorting with young people. They help them separate what truly matters, what requires their attention here and now, as opposed to what is simply a distraction from what is truly essential. When our students and children come to us, as they often do, with a cluttered and frenzied list of what is "stressing them out," the most helpful assistance from a calm and non-flustered adult will be to help them deter-mine what is truly pivotal and requiring their attention, both at that very moment and for the long term.

Such sorting is becoming an increasingly important need for all of us in our contemporary world. As British theologian David Ford describes it, our culture suffers from an "addiction to urgency."[34] Matters both large and small come at us with equal intensity, demanding from us im-mediate responses. The number of emails we receive with the red exclamation points beside them, identifying those messages as "urgent," grows with each passing day. Sitting with young people, helping them to sort out what truly matters from what can wait, is a crucial task that only a discerning and patient adult can help them to do.

As I approached my senior year in high school, I went with my father on a number of visits to college campuses. Looking back on those visits, I see they were pivotal and formative moments in our relationship, as well as times of important self-discovery for me. In subsequent years I have heard countless parents talk with great tenderness and gratitude of these times, if for no other reason than that they afforded a chance for conversation as the parents trav-eled with their child and went on admissions tours. On a visit we paid to Franklin and Marshall College in Pennsyl-vania, I met alone with the Director of Admissions and he asked me about all of the activities I was involved in as a high school student. Having quite an impressive array of extracurricular activities, I proudly went through my list and described each one. Seemingly undeterred by this ex-tensive list, he then went on to ask me, "And which of those are the most important to you?"

I was completely caught off guard by that question; it had never before occurred to me that some endeavors might have priority over others. In my adolescent view of the world, the value lay in the number and extent of those involvements, yet here was an adult asking me to give them priority and value. While it was a jolting question, and my contact with this wonderful adult was limited to about an hour of conversation with a very nice follow-up note from him, it was a transformative moment for me. Not surprisingly, I have found myself asking that type of question to a great many young people, especially during my own stint as an admissions director. Moreover, whenever I have encountered graduates of Franklin and Marshall College in the ensuing years and shared that experience, virtually all of them knew immediately, without my naming him, the man in question. Clearly, he had posed similar questions to all of them, no doubt helping to shape a great many lives in the process.

---

(3) Always ask at least one more question.

In reflecting on my growing up years, I have been struck by the fact that some of the most important moments of learning and self-discovery occurred when an adult posed a question to me. It turns out—much to my surprise—that the answers I have found for myself in life have come as a result of the questions some key adults dared to ask me.

As a college student, I found myself taking my independent study project far too seriously. With my topic being the philosopher Martin Heidegger and his view of death, it is not hard to see how such intense study of very dense and complex writing could land me in such a state. Sharing my anguish with my advisor one morning, he was both patient with me and understanding of how these immense and murky matters could bring, in Heidegger's view, a sense of existential angst to my life. At one point, following a period of silence, he looked at me and addressed not the issue of Heidegger but something seemingly far from the agenda at hand. "How is your love life?" he asked me in all seriousness. It is not hard to imagine how much the question surprised me, and I mumbled something ambiguous in reply.

Yet I can clearly remember the look on his face when he asked: this was no effort to lighten up the conversation or sidestep the issues at hand. There was a genuine link, and in retrospect I see that he sensed something in me, though beneath the surface, that was real, profound, and closely intertwined with my angst.

This was a professor who had clearly sat with other students anguished over the progress or content of their work and had, through such questions, brought them back home. Thanks to his willingness to ask that question, I was able to begin to perceive how my intense involvement in my studies had a connection to how I was dealing with matters of intimacy in my life. It may not be appropriate to ask such a direct or intimate question much of the time (it is obviously not a question appropriate for parents to ask, for example), but when an adult is willing to probe more deeply beneath the surface and help young people make connections they might otherwise miss, it is of great service in helping them think about and make sense of their lives.

In a world that does not sit easily with a sustained period of questioning, our normal mode of operation is to jump into action or response, seeking what one writer calls "premature clarity."[35] So lingering with the concern of a young person, asking her at least one more question (perhaps one that will take her by surprise), is something that demands great courage, not to mention a good deal of time. The value to the young person, however, is enormous. On virtually every occasion when I have opted to ask a student just one more question—be it to clarify something already said or to bring up a related perspective—my understanding of his needs were either broadened or changed. The offering of yet one more question will often change his perspective as well, helping him to see the whole situation in a different light.

Recently I paid a visit to Virginia Episcopal School in Lynchburg, where the student leaders had been giving some serious thought to the core values of the institution. These students initially identified seven core values, which they then narrowed down to three: integrity, maturity, and drive. I was intrigued that the students had focused on maturity—*lack* of maturity is something that young people quickly identify, but a positive view of maturity is more rare. When I asked the dean of students about it, his response stuck with me: "I believe they saw it as the ability to pull back from the moment." One of the true signs of maturity is to do such pulling back from the moment: just when we are ready to pronounce our judgment on what a child or student has done, or when we find ourselves reacting in anger or confusion, it is wise to pull back from the moment. And I have found that one of the greatest aids to "pulling back" is asking one more question.

---

(4) No matter how shocked you might be, don't show it.

Among those moments when I have felt most effective in my work with young people, the times when I have been able to handle their issues with as little drama as possible stand out. I have heard, over the years, some pretty bizarre and surprising things, so the fact that I have simply come to expect it has allowed me to exhibit less shock, regardless of how jolted I may be on the inside. There is a real link between our ability not to appear to be caught off guard and how effective we can be as adults.

This is not to say that we should not treat the matter as anything but serious, nor seek to avoid speaking to the depth of the challenge a young person might be facing. It is particularly hard for parents not to overreact; after all, we are talking about one's own flesh and blood. But frequently young people, be they students or our own children, bring problems to us as much to see the reaction they might get as to seek solutions to the problem.

There was a period in my own adolescence when I had the habit of bringing problems to various people—teachers, clergy, doctors—on a regular basis. Perhaps I was searching for that one person who could truly listen to my quandaries, or I might well have been seeking out models that would help me as I thought through my aspirations. What I remember as most helpful about those many conversations is not the advice those people gave me, but the degree to which they treated my problems with calmness and normalcy. While no doubt they had heard such problems many times before, the most helpful adults regarded the situations I presented to them as both unique and thoroughly human. That, in retrospect, was what I was looking for: a reaction that told me I was not bizarre or sick, yet did not discount my uncertainties as either trivial or "just a phase." It turns out that what is pivotal to the dilemmas presented to us by young people is how we react to them as much as how we help solve them, and our ability neither to trivialize nor panic is a crucial help as young people seek to understand their actions and the motivations behind them.

---

(5) Nothing is more important for a young person than to be taken seriously by an adult who remains an adult.

In years past, when I have been perplexed by the behavior or attitude of a student, I have always found my first conversation with the parents to be instructive. Sometimes they are able to tell me things about their son or daughter that shed new light on the things I have seen. At other times what they have *not* said sheds as much light on the matter as what they have said. Just as we never roam that far away from our parents' attitudes and reactions, so we can learn a lot about the young from their parents.

Julius was a young man who seemed to be spending an inordinate amount of time talking with faculty members at the school where I worked. The faculty and I noticed, in his initial weeks at the school, that he seemed to feel much more comfortable around adults than his peers—hardly an uncommon thing among young people today. He would joke with us, process an idea or theory with us, or simply seem to want to be in our company. At times, of course, his clinging to us would drive us crazy. We also knew it was not good for his relationships with the other students: the more his peers saw of this, the more they tended to distance themselves.

When I first met with Julius's parents, I began to understand why Julius had such a need to be around the adults in the school. They admitted that Julius spent a great deal of time on his own, but I also sensed that they really did not pay much attention to Julius when they were in his company. When I would mention something he had said to me, they were quick to discount his viewpoint, calling him immature and naïve.

There is no greater blessing for the young than to discover, at various junctures in their lives, that they are interesting to adults, that their opinions, their understandings of life, their emerging sense of humor and irony are things the important adults in their life both enjoy and take seriously. For this to take place, however, it is vital that the boundaries between adult and young person are maintained. For when we adults descend to a youthful level of behavior and humor, we forfeit the distance needed to help young persons see that their lives matter to an adult. Similarly, when we talk down to young people in a condescending or patronizing manner, we also compromise that essential distance, depriving them of the opportunity to share a part of their lives with an adult. Likewise, it keeps us from finding both interest and meaning in what they are saying.

Humor is vital in the lives of children as they grow into adulthood. Having a good sense of humor is a cherished and much-envied attribute among the young, as is the ability to make adults laugh. It tells young people that their sense of humor transcends the juvenile, allows them to feel a certain sense of power, and shows them that we enjoy them and take them seriously. Granted, the conversation may be far from serious; nonetheless, humor is serious business among the young! In thinking about the most influential adults in my life, I can see all of them at some point or another truly enjoying the humor of the young without relinquishing their role as an adult. The realization that the young can touch our funny bone, as well as our mind and soul, is an uncommon gift, and is a key component in that young person finding the world of adulthood to be in any way appealing.

LEARNING FROM THE YOUNG

As Erik Erikson once reminded us, "The fashionable insistence on dramatizing the dependence of children on adults often blinds us to the dependence of the older generation on the younger one."[36] Indeed, to be a teacher is constantly to be learning from one's students, while parents routinely report that having children is the biggest learning experience of their lives. Influence, it turns out, works both ways. The upcoming generation is an immense help to adults who are trying to understand what it means to be an adult. As long as we are able to remain adults as we learn from our children and our students, we receive the gift not only of remaining young, in one sense, but of maturing and growing into wisdom.

Accordingly, here are some of the practical things I have learned from young people, both about myself as an adult and in the service of caring better for them as future adults.

---

(1) The value of time.

Nothing is more precious to our society today than time. It is the all-pervasive issue in so many of our lives. It may be the problem of families carving out enough time for themselves in the midst of so many competing demands, or, in the words of one highly respected school head, "the feeling that there is never enough time for what really matters."[37] The constant pinch of having to squeeze too much into too little time is a sure sign, as Carl Jung reminded us, of the presence of anxiety in our lives.

Those stark realities do not hinder young people from expecting time from us, and as full as their lives may be they still need to know that key adults in their lives will make time for them. Accordingly, I feel I am doing my work well when I am able to give young people the sense that I have more time on my hands than they do. This became clear to me when I worked on a college campus, where time is both a precious commodity as well as a problem: how do I use and structure all of that time? As I would meet students on the crosswalk, our conversations were entirely different if I was not in a rush to be at the next place, regardless of how much of a rush the student was in at the time. Likewise, when I took more causal strolls around the high school where I served, I noticed things more than when I was in a rush to be somewhere else. It *does* make a difference what mental and emotional state we are in, and how we deal with the pressures of time.

An experienced and highly regarded teacher came to my office one day prior to Christmas break. He explained his plight to me: "Today I have had a steady string of former students coming to my office unexpectedly, and without letting me know in advance. Here they want me to spend time with them, and yet I have a hundred tasks I need to complete before the end of the week!" It is a poignant example of the plight of a good teacher, as well as the reality that our young people need sheer time from us. The more we have to give to them, the greater our influence will be. There is no guarantee that they will respond to us in the time we intentionally set aside for them—in fact, I have discovered that there is no connection between the two at all!—and sometimes we have to drop everything and tend to them, something very difficult for all of us. As busy as young people may seem today, when it comes to their need for adults, they seek that time and seek our availability.

(2) The value of absence.

One of the problems of adhering to the ideal of "being there for our children" is the assumption that this means being literally, physically present. It is at the root of what we refer to as "helicopter parenting," those parents who physically hover over their children well into their early adult years. To be close to our children, we think we need to be physically there as much of the time as possible.

Our children do need our physical presence a great deal of the time; simply "showing up" can make a great difference in their lives. However, our children also need our absence, although in a world of "being there" for others, such a value may seem heretical. In fact, they need our absence as much as our presence: otherwise the voices we seek to instill in them and the images we want them to carry from us will not have a chance to flourish. Today young people are so used to being able to get in touch with their parents immediately—in part a sign of our concern about their safety—that they can be deprived of the opportunity to reflect on the matter at hand and come to some difficult decisions on their own.

Wherever I have served in a school or college, I have always felt slightly guilty whenever I had to be away from the campus or grounds of the school. My need to be needed, of course, was being severely tested, and images of great calamities occurring during my absence would flare up in my head and heart. Absence, however, has taught me some important lessons, for frequently in my absence problems were solved, not left to fester. A student who emailed me to say that she "just had to see me right now" was actually able to take care of the situation on her own. A student who was going through a difficult emotional period turned out not only to be just fine in my absence, but perhaps even felt better and solved a problem on his own. I was also frequently amazed and even humbled when an urgent problem communicated via email would then be resolved in my absence. While such realities can be a blow to the ego, it does remind us of the value of not always being around, for it allows young people the much-needed opportunity to work through something on their own.

As Henri Nouwen once wrote, the most helpful guide "is the one who, instead of advising what to do or to whom to go, offers us the chance to stay alone and take the risk of entering into our own experience."[38] The need to be needed always requires reality checks, and one of those checks is the ability to recognize the times when we are *not* needed, when the best thing we could do is to leave the young person alone. We need to be reminded of what our goal is with our children and students: that they will be able, in the long run, to adjust and thrive as independent adults. That simply cannot happen if we are always hovering around them, ready and eager to solve whatever problem they pose to us along the way. Their internal voices will not have the chance to develop.

---

(3) The value of silence.

During my visits to school chapels across the country, I am often moved by the experience of silence in worship. Some school chapels in this country are incorporating a pro-longed period of silence into chapel services, particularly with high school students, and school chaplains report that students are not only able to cope with it, but are eager for it. As one chaplain told me at the beginning of the school year, a number of students had reported to her that one of the things they most missed about school over the summer was the opportunity for silence in the context of chapel. Quaker schools have known for quite some time the role that silence plays in worship, but the hurried, media-soaked world of young people does not often allow space for the absence of words or music. Yet the soul of the young person in fact longs for it.

If nothing else, silence provides for young people a way out of the noise of their lives into some of the richness and depth that the adult world can offer. Young people are so-phisticated enough to know just what the onslaught of the media does to and wants from them; what fewer know is the availability and redemptive value of silence as a pow-erful and fertile means of seeing beyond the havoc that can characterize their lives. Whether they use it for prayer, re-flection, or at times a half-sleep, it lends confirmation to the fact that they indeed have souls and are quite capable of delving into them.

Silence is something I have also come to understand as valuable in the classroom. Whether it be a pause in what I am saying, a pause after a good question has been asked, or, most frequently, a pause following a question I ask myself, silence is a rich tool for learning. It reminds both teacher and student of the place of reflection in the process of learning, something that so many of our educational institutions seem to be forgetting.

Students have taught me a very important lesson about silence over the years. Let's say I have asked a question in class but no one leaps to answer it. A nervous and uncertain pause ensues and, like most teachers, I am tempted to rephrase the question, call on a particular student, or move on. Or perhaps I ask a student something in a counseling session, and as she hesitates, I feel the tinge of discomfort known to all of us at an unexpected silence. Yet be it in a classroom or in conversation, silence is no automatic indicator of the absence of a response; it is more often a prelude, an indication of the young person processing through and being on the cusp of articulating a response. Frequently some of the most poignant answers I have received from students come when I allow them the luxury of a few moments of silence. In class it can result in some discomfort, as students look around the room to see if anyone is courageous enough to answer and thereby break this intolerable impasse. That silence, nonetheless, provides them a model of difference; they see that the adult standing or sitting there is comfortable with a realm that they know little of but may well be attracted to in the process of understanding this adult world.

---

(4) The value of a sense of occasion.

One of the saddest symptoms of the contemporary malaise of our culture is the decline in understanding a sense of occasion. We have forgotten that different times and contexts demand from us different responses and behaviors. Hence, we talk to each other in movie theaters as if we were home watching a DVD, we speak on cell phones in public places as if we were in private, and we dress the same way for one event in our lives as for all others. No doubt the blurring of home and work, of leisure and labor, has facilitated some of this decline, but I would also add that our increasing privatization as a society has also been a contributing factor. We simply know less and less about how to act and be in a public place.

Over the years I have spoken in many school assemblies or chapels across the country, in both sectarian and non-sectarian institutions. It strikes me how easy it is to see the difference between a group of students experienced in listening to a speaker and gathering in a common place and a group that is not. The quality of listening is better: a speaker can sense when the audience is schooled in the art of coming together and listening as a group. The unspoken but shared sense of what a gathering of this sort demands is deeper, and the capacity of students to ask intelligent and focused follow-up questions is stronger. There is something that develops in young people as they practice, so to speak, this act of coming together as a group of people as opposed to being a mere collection of individuals.

Some adults may find this sense of occasion to be superficial, assuming it has to do with the traditional niceties of dressing up, being polite, or paying attention. An interactive world, as we know it, may call for new rules and new assumptions. I would maintain, however, that developing a sense of occasion—one that does not exclude niceties but also addresses our need for commitment to something beyond us—is both a much-needed way to show respect for the common spaces of life and allows young people to understand the complexities of adult life. Different occasions demand different preparations and responses; therein lies a distinctive and—I believe—appealing difference between the domain of the adult and the domain of the young.

(5) The value of face-to-face contact.

As one writer reminds us, while the contemporary world allows us to be in long-distance touch with other people in lots of efficient and ingenious ways, the need for people-to-people contact is greater now than ever before.[39] Our temptation is to assume that a phone call or email will suffice in our efforts to keep in touch with those around us. Such reliance, it turns out, makes the direct, face-to-face interaction with people even more necessary.

One headmaster I knew was fond of saying that often he would use a lavatory across the campus just so he could get out and around the school, making face-to-face contact with students and teachers and absorbing the atmosphere and mood. I can attest to the value of that. Every time I have left the office and taken a walk in the middle of the day, without exception, I have found myself engaging in important conversations I never expected to have. If parents occasionally roamed around the home when the family is there, with no specific purpose in mind, it might have some surprising results. It is true that young people will often share thoughts or ideas with their elders in emails that they might not in person, but bringing up a problem and talking about it can often best be done when you are in the same room. The sense of presence that we spoke of earlier, so needed by young people in their parents and teachers, can only occur through showing up and being visible. I can get a great deal done through email and telephone access to others, but I cannot capture the immediacy and the value that being physically present to young people can be.

The lives of adults are abundant with models of how we have made sense of this grown-up world from childhood on. The deeper we dig into our lives, the more we learn about the place of adults in our own world and how so many of them have helped shape the complex people we are today. Yet another surprise may come to us as we do this digging: going through our memories and our influences over the years may make us yearn to deepen and expand the connections we discover there, extending them to the ultimate source and creator of those connections. In doing so we have begun to tread upon the spiritual lives of adults, and that dimension of our exploration now looms clearly before us.

six

TOURIST OR PILGRIM?

Digging Deeper for Courage and Hope

One of the saddest things in the world is to see a cynical young person. Because it means that he or she has gone from knowing nothing to believing nothing.

> —*Maya Angelou,*
> *interview, Academy of Achievement*
> *(January 1997)*

How many parents think of themselves as God's agents and representatives for their children when they hear them cry at 3:30 a.m. or when they break up warring siblings for the tenth time in one morning?

> —*Douglas Schuurman,*
> Vocation

IF I WERE ASKED to describe in one or two words our contemporary way of living, I would say *in motion*. Always on the go, always "moving forward," we view ourselves, indeed experience ourselves, as beings in motion, frequently running behind, almost always hurried, and feeling the fatigue that results from this perpetual movement.

It is hard not to feel trapped in this constant motion, but it has been helpful for me to remember an important distinction I read about some years ago. In an essay called "Pilgrims and Pioneers," Richard R. Niebuhr writes of the difference between being a tourist in life and being a pilgrim. Tourists are those who "dabble," making their rounds and traveling into new territory, but not allowing that territory in any way to change or move them. When we are tourists we attempt to keep the serious things we encounter along the way at arm's length. When we are pilgrims, on the other hand, we make our rounds with a purpose, and allow the terrain we cover to move us, indeed to change us. As pilgrims we see things, interpret what we see, and can potentially be influenced by these experiences. As a result, there is an "enlargement of ourselves" when we are pilgrims, an opportunity that touring simply does not provide.[40]

As we venture forth into this terrain called adulthood, frequently experiencing unfamiliar and strange new lands, are we allowing these experiences to influence and ultimately transform us, or are we simply dabbling? That is the spiritual question I would like to pose.

Anyone who ventures forth wearing a clerical collar in public can tell you many stories of how people react upon seeing this sign of the church's presence. On occasions it immediately opens doors and prompts acts of generosity and respect; I remember an elderly man in Boston offering to give up his seat for me on a crowded bus, and sometimes complete strangers will initiate thoughtful conversations with a priest or pastor on an airplane. But on other occasions the sight of a clerical collar evokes suspicion and hostility, as someone's experience of God or the church brings a look of disdain or anger. This outward symbol of something mysterious and ineffable can disarm some people, while arming others.

Another reaction, however, occurs with surprising frequency. Let's say I am on an elevator, and it stops at a floor to pick up two additional passengers. They board the elevator, joking with each other; then when they catch sight of me, they quietly begin to laugh. I can only imagine what they must be thinking: "If this 'man of the cloth' only knew what we were talking about just a minute ago!" To them, I may represent all that is traditional, formal, mannered, and—dare I say—adult. In turn, they might very well see themselves as being the opposite—fresh, spontaneous, slightly risqué, and very informal. They are proud to be "out of the box" types of people, having cast aside the formality of the past in favor of a more youthful way of being.

At the same time, I know such people also need adults like me—and what we seem to represent on the surface—in order for them to revel in their distinctiveness. All of the images I evoke of rectitude and stuffiness provide an essential foil for their youthful high spirits. I represent the "box" they are proud to be out of. An increasing number of adults, I sense, like to define themselves as brash, even rowdy, "out there," saying what is on their mind regardless of what others might think. Yet, just like adolescents, they also need an "other," a symbol of what is traditional, formal, and mannered, against which they can rebel. How can one feel the thrill of being rowdy if there is no concept of decorum prevailing? What is the fun of being shocking if there is no one around to be shocked? In a world in which we are increasingly prone to shun tradition and public commitments, to define ourselves as tourists as opposed to pilgrims, we still seem to need traditions or institutions against which we can define ourselves to the contrary. As one school head observed, "There seem to be an increasing number of parents feeling free to 'sound off' (a version of what the media loves to refer to as 'speaking out') without any sense of accountability for what they say." Indeed, to "sound off" in this way requires a listener who represents the other side.

That is the dilemma of the serious adult today, who is under fire from both adolescents and other grown-ups. As teachers, we may feel a sense of rebellion from many parents and other adults against what we stand for, and yet we are deeply needed. Today parents feel permission to criticize or accuse teachers in increasingly adolescent ways, yet at the same time they need those teachers to preserve their sense of decorum, to listen to their venting, and to respond in a calm and non-reactive fashion. No wonder that teachers, like clergy, are the "professional adults" in our culture:[41] they hold the line in a fashion that is both traditional and predictable, thereby allowing many parents to assume a more juvenile role. Perhaps we assume we can get away with keeping only one part of what Freud referred to as the unhappy truce human beings reach with the concept of civilization: we seek the protection of a culture of restraint without its limitations on our own forms of behavior and expression.[42]

It is often these same adults who differentiate spirituality from religion, and in defining themselves as "spiritual, but not religious" claim to hold on to the "best" of religion—its depth, its seriousness about things that matter, its attention to the inner life—without dealing with the "worst" of religion—its tendency to become dogmatic, rigid, moralistic, and institution-bound. We are now well into the second generation of what has been called an age of "religious illiteracy,"[43] in which many adults function without a working religious vocabulary or much content knowledge of religious traditions. When you ask these adults what they mean when they say they are "spiritual, but not religious," you will frequently be met with a vague response, such as, "I can commune with God on a golf course as much as in church," or "I feel God is within me, not out there in some institution." Their spirituality is not bolstered by a particular pattern of spiritual practice or a sense of commitment to something larger than themselves. It frequently sounds like a "dabbling" in the life of the spirit, as opposed to allowing that life and practice to have an impact on them. In fact, words like "dogma" or "doctrine" or "institutional religion" tend to be heard negatively, with the concluding response, "I don't want anyone telling me what to believe." These interpretations help the speaker to view herself as less judgmental, more inclusive, and more open than a more dogmatic or "religious" person.

Religion, in other words, is viewed as an overly adult—and overly restrictive—form of believing in God. When we combine the tendency of adults today to eschew traditional notions of maturity with their lack of understanding of what religion can mean, it is not hard to see why many are at best distrustful of its value and at worst outright hostile to its expectations. There is no doubt, as well, that some of the suspicious and angry looks I get when I am wearing a clerical collar stem from spiritual wounds inflicted in the past by those who were in power and seeking control.

Perhaps I have been unusually fortunate in my own experience of religion, because I see it as less about wielding power and more as a vehicle for accountability, constantly balanced alongside the infinite capacity of God to forgive and help us to begin anew. To me, the religious life is made up of practice, rhythm, grace, story, and moral choice. It also means community, a community that does not swallow up our individuality but welcomes it, all the while providing for each one of us a much needed connection to something beyond ourselves. The working out of that pattern of life and connection with others is as much about coming to terms with our own humanity as our spirituality. As the Roman Catholic theologian Teilhard de Chardin was fond of putting it, we are not human beings on a spiritual journey, we are spiritual beings on a human journey. At the same time, however, I realize that this view of religion may be a long way from what many adults have experienced, and may represent a diminishing "center" in our culture of extremes.

This perspective does not generate a lot of heat and light; it can even be viewed as rather dull. I recall one panel I served on as a college chaplain on the subject of same-sex marriages, and in the question-and-answer session all the audience wished to do was challenge the viewpoint of the most conservative panelist there. The same, I suspect, would go for a conservative audience challenging a liberal viewpoint. If hot debate is what is desired, it is more easily done with those who convey the message in the boldest possible strokes. It might be that the sound-bite culture in which we live does not welcome nuance or complexity.

As with the boisterous adults on the elevator, such audiences need a certain notion of authority (or lack of it) against which they can define themselves. Perhaps it made that audience in the panel discussion feel affirmed in their liberal views to challenge the conservative viewpoint; no doubt conservatives would feel the same. Defining ourselves against the grain elevates our sense of self and what we feel to be of value in life. To define ourselves in opposition to what we perceive as a close-minded and rigid approach to religion—at whatever end of the spectrum— allows us to rest easier with those rigidities and premature conclusions in our own lives. In other words, as much as the religious realm can be an escape from the responsibilities and ambiguities of adulthood, so those who define themselves in opposition to religion may also be evading the demands of adulthood. In casting off the staid and institutional, we can avoid the demands of moral seriousness, stability, and commitment.

Fewer and fewer people these days know how to behave when they are inside a house of worship. Like many clergy, I see the symptoms of this distrust of institutionalized religion most often at marriages and funerals, where those who are "unchurched" are most likely to have to deal with it. The visits many people today make to houses of worship are more akin to a tourist stop. People seem more reluctant to enter a church until the very last moment—the less time spent inside the better!—hence a crowd inevitably gathers outside the church. Movie portrayals of weddings and funerals almost always include some element of shock (the bride left at the altar, the corpse sitting up in the coffin) or a total disregard for a sense of decorum.

Not all adults who are serious about this maturity business, who seek to influence children and youth in ways by which they can more fully enter into adulthood on their own, are going to gravitate toward religion. On the other hand, however, we are seeing today an increasing comfort level—among both young people and their elders—with the idea of spirituality. So it is my hope that an intensified conversation regarding what adult spirituality entails, and how that spirituality enables us to be pilgrims, not just tourists, will go a long way toward helping grown-ups guide young people and speak to the fullness of those emerging internal selves. Accordingly, my question is this: *In what ways can a spiritual vision encourage and enable us to be better adults to our sons, daughters, and students, in the hope that they in turn can grow into the adults we want them to be and wish ourselves to be?* In response, I have a few observations to offer.

---

(1) A spiritual vision can help us better
say "yes" and "no" in life.

By "yes" and "no" I refer to the decisions we make regarding what is truly important in life. I mean the "non-negotiables" of our lives, particularly as they relate to guiding young people, the grounds upon which we make so many of our day-to-day decisions and which may, at times, force us to say "no" to things that are more appealing but less important in the long run. There is no more important element of the spiritual life than this process of valuing, of learning to decide what deserves our time, attention, and energy. Moreover, this kind of discernment does more than anything else to define us as adults, both in terms of our self-awareness and in how we function as grown-ups. As author Shawn Copeland puts it, "Saying yes and saying no are companions in the process of constituting a whole and holy life."[44]

For example, as a teenager I often found myself fixated on externals, such as the type of car that my parents drove. I found myself impatient with their reluctance to purchase a more expensive car, as so many of my friends' parents had done, and I pleaded with them to "upgrade" to a better model of car. They refused, but they did so for a reason: my parents had made it clear that I should choose whatever college I attended based not on cost but on where I most wanted to go. They would take care of the costs. As the years have passed, I have become increasingly aware of the powerful message my parents sent to me: there were some things that mattered, and other things were less pressing. While they had said "yes" to saving for my college education, they knew that involved saying "no" to some of the things that beguiled me during those teenage years—perhaps even things like cars or vacations they would have themselves enjoyed.

It is vitally important that we view this process of saying "yes" and saying "no" as being within the realm of the spiritual, if for no other reason than the fact that it is such a difficult and draining activity today, requiring all of our spiritual resources and convictions. To identify and separate what it truly urgent from what merely masquerades as being urgent among the many things calling for our attention today is a spiritual practice. In defining boundaries and making choices, we are engaged in a process of determining what is truly most important and fundamental in life. These choices will in turn infuse our lives with meaning and courage. There are so few supports today for those who attempt to set limits—in our own lives as well as in the lives of our children and students—that we are forced to draw upon the deepest of our longings and hopes in life. We need reasons—substantial reasons—for drawing the boundaries of our lives and the lives of our young people.

Most difficult of all in this process of saying "yes" and saying "no" is the effect on our self-esteem. We all need to be liked, to have our children or students depend on us, to appear invincible and powerful, to be viewed as "with it" and in touch, in synch with the younger generation. Setting limits, determining when to say "yes" and when to say "no" in our lives, can leave us feeling drained, worried that we are too rigid, curmudgeonly, or outmoded. The attraction of remaining in step with the young is simply too strong in our culture for taking stands simply as a strategy or mode of last resort.

Here is an example. One spring I received word that the senior class of the school—all seventy-five of them—was planning to cut school in order to revive an old custom in the school called "Senior Skip Day." The particular day they had chosen was an especially bad day to revive this custom, with major tests as well as athletic events being held. It was also far too early in the springtime for seniors to be taking such liberties; what was in store for us for the rest of the semester? Moreover, they had not lived up to their agreement with me to plan this skip day well in advance so that we could determine just how feasible it would be.

When the senior class president called me the night before to announce it, I told him in no uncertain terms that I expected to see the seniors attending class the next day. As morning arrived, there were no seniors to be found anywhere. Then I got word that all of them were in the school library, prepared to take their leave of campus for the rest of the day. I immediately headed over, not knowing what I would find and wondering just what I would do if the students did not go along with my orders. After all, there were seventy-five of them and only one of me! Even worse, I found myself full of self-doubt. Was I being too "draconian" in holding the line, or provoking an unnecessary showdown that could well result in my looking foolish and losing the seniors' respect? (After all, as one school head told me, "On paper, the odds are always against us: there are more of them than us, and they are bigger than we are. We are forced to rely only on our moral authority, and that is it.") My doubts gave way to a sense of desperation, and I heard myself saying, "God, just get me through this."

When I faced the entire senior class in the library, their backpacks stocked for a day at the beach, I told them that this was not a legitimate skip day and that I expected them to head to their morning classes. There was no response, only resentful stares. "Any questions?" I asked them. Not one. I turned around and headed back for my office without the least idea of what would transpire. Much to their credit, the students went to their classes, although I was hardly the most popular authority figure in their lives that day or for days to come, and some of their parents complained that I was being too strict. In the long run, however, I sensed those students needed someone to set some limits and the rest of the year they were terrific as a class.

A few years later, our basketball team had a game with a nearby rival school marked by tension throughout the contest between the opposing crowds. While we got through the game without an incident, I worried about what might occur afterward on the grounds of the school or somewhere nearby in Northwest Washington. Heading out the door of the gymnasium, I saw before me two rival groups of students facing off, with fists waving and bodies being shoved at the very center. Four students—two from each school—began to fight. Without stopping to think I tore into the center of the action, into the middle of the fight, and broke up the impending battle.

Growing up, I had carefully managed to avoid fights, partly due to my own easygoing personality and partly to my fear of losing. I could not imagine a situation I would rather avoid, and I hardly felt equipped to jump into the midst of a fistfight and break it up. Compared to the strong and agile students squaring off that evening, I had little chance of holding my own. Yet without thinking I plunged into the middle of the battle, separating one student from another by force. Looking back on that event, I cannot believe to this day that I actually did what I did; my natural inclination clearly would have been to head in the opposite direction.

Whether we are a parent or a teacher, we all know those moments when we have deep self-doubt about our ability to set limits. We wonder what will happen if those students or children just ignore us and do what they want to do. We feel isolated in such situations, having nothing at our disposal except our sheer moral authority—for what that may be worth! At other times we just do what we have to do and wonder, in retrospect, how in the world did we get through it all?

As much as we loathe them, however, these are—as hard as it may be to imagine—sacred moments. They are sacred not because of the exercise of our adult power or control, but because we have had to draw upon our deepest resources. At such times, when we have to rely on our own sense of ourselves as mature adults, distinct from young people, we are responding out of inner conviction for their sakes. It takes all of the courage and rising above self-doubt we can muster. These are the moments that are rarely talked about in the self-help books on parenting or teaching—they do not fit easily into self-help tips—yet these above all others are the moments that define who we are as adults. It takes an enormous amount of sheer will and fortitude to get through them, and we may surprise ourselves that we actually had it in us to do what the occasion demanded. In standing our ground, we stand on holy ground.

True, we may also draw upon our stubbornness and rigidity at such moments, but—once again—our students and children need to see us drawing the lines. In turn, they will have to stand their ground against big odds in their own adult lives. What internal models will they be able to draw upon in order to do the right thing? The plaintive cry, "God, get me through this!" turns out to be a telling sign of just what these moments are all about.

---

(2) A spiritual vision will allow us to develop a language and context for sacrifice.

At least before the recent worldwide economic crisis, few Americans were prepared to consider a significant change in the way they lived. As the historian Livy wrote of ancient Rome, "We have reached the point where we cannot bear either our vices or their cure."[45] While our condition as a society may not be that of ancient Rome, Americans seem to be trapped in a bind of disliking both the symptoms and the solutions. Survey after survey indicate that a great many of us feel the country is going in the wrong direction, yet are we ready to assume the burden of redirecting our country? To do so would force us to look at the ways in which we are going to have to sacrifice, and we are far from ready to embrace that activity.

To help heal our environment, to bring our planet back from great duress and calamity, and to deal with a diminished economy, we need to think about the ways that individuals and societies are going to have to sacrifice some of our luxuries and patterns of living for the good of the larger order. Recent economic downturns may well put an end to many of our cherished hopes for the future, and alter our images of what constitutes "the good life" in the years ahead. Yet secular culture lacks a substantial vocabulary for a notion of the sort of sacrifice that is urgently needed to meet the enormous challenges ahead of us.

As I heard Professor Mary Evelyn Tucker observe to a group of school chaplains and teachers of religion, "You are unique in our society, in that you have at your disposal a language of sacrifice." Furthermore, having a spiritual vision allows an individual the opportunity to see that when something breaks down, something is also emerging.[46] The religious traditions of our culture hold a reservoir of words, images, and stories that help us not only to make sense of the sacrifices that lie ahead of us, but also give us a spiritual vision of hope amid sacrifice. New things emerge: sacrifice does not mean simply giving up but also opening the door to new and redemptive modes of living. It involves, as Richard Luov has suggested, a spiritual take on the world that "looks far beyond our own generational needs" to the welfare of future generations.[47]

Are we preparing our children for what lies ahead of them? Do they understand the notion of sacrifice, and how it may be operative in their adult lives? It is no good simply to remind the young of what the future may hold, to plant the responsibility for cleaning up our messes on their shoulders; we also need to equip them to face it. We are the ones that got them into this quagmire, so it is incumbent upon us to provide adult models of sacrifice, letting them see us giving up things that matter to us for the sake of the common good. The longer we wait to embrace this notion of sacrifice, the less equipped our children will be to undertake and endure the sacrifices they will experience in turn.

As I listen to parents speak about some of their deepest fears for their children, a recurring theme emerges. It has to do with their worry that their sons or daughters will not experience the standard of living they themselves have enjoyed. It is a frightening thing for a parent to contemplate; it cuts deep into our basic longings for our children, that they lead happy lives full of choice and abundance. I believe it is at the heart of our growing frenzy over admission to college, not to mention to the schools and preschools that precede it. If there will be fewer pieces of the pie available in the years ahead, some parents may reason, why not position my sons and daughters in a way that will most likely insure a secure future? If sacrifice is inevitable, why not strive to set the stage as best we can for a life that will require the minimum sacrifice necessary, insulated from what so many others will have to endure? So we go to great lengths to make certain that the avenues we think will lead to that good life, however diminished in the future, will be open to them.

At the same time, we have pitched the stakes for young people and their success so high that relatively small setbacks can seem calamitous, way out of proportion to their long-term health and success. Parents can blame a school for being too harsh, a coach for not playing their son or daughter more in the games, a system that did not get their child into the college of her dreams. One setback—painful and discouraging as it may be—carries with it, in the eyes of many parents, the potential of doing infinite harm to the offspring, leading us into what Madeline Levine refers to as "a tizzy of despair way out of proportion to reality."[48] Concern over the poor grade at semester's end escalates into anxiety over a poor grade on an individual test; keeping a child back to repeat a grade can be viewed as unthinkable even if it is recommended by the school as in the best interests of the child. Larger disappointments and setbacks are robbed of their educational and developmental value. Small things become huge in a blur of worry that one small misstep will ruin the entire plan.

A plan that may no longer be viable, ambition for a son or daughter that may have more to do with what the parent wants than the child, a view of the world that says if you play the game in a certain way you will end up ahead, a desire to conform to what is seen as success—such dreams may need to be relinquished for the good of the child. It is the only way a child will learn to deal with the sacrifices that lie ahead. For our own sake, as well as the sake of our children, we must, in the words of Robert Coles, "accept times of surrender before life's thickness, its complexities, ironies, ambiguities, and its chancy nature."[49]

As with many educators who have worked with young people over the years, I have found that the most powerful moments in that work emerge when students are coming to terms with reduced expectations of themselves: *I let myself or others down; I thought I could do all that I had taken on; I can't believe I screwed up in the way I did.* Those are tremendously painful but poignant experiences, and while they feel like severe setbacks at the time, they have the power to mold all of us into the deeper human beings we can become.

---

(3) The spiritual vision is about taking in the larger perspective and savoring what it has to offer us.

Recently, on the last page of the Summer 2008 issue of the *Kent School Bulletin*, I saw a photograph of a school chapel that impressed me as both soothing and haunting. The picture was not featuring a chapel full of people, or an empty chapel of great architectural beauty. Instead, it showed a few people sitting in the chapel, while a sense of quiet pervaded. Perhaps they had arrived early, well ahead of the others, and were waiting for a big service to begin that would infuse the space with a very different mood. Alternatively, perhaps these few people had chosen to linger after the big event was over, to relish what they had just experienced or simply wait for the crowds to thin out before heading to the next event. Whatever the context, there was an odd but powerful stillness about the photograph; it seemed to suggest that those who had either arrived early or were lingering in the aftermath were savoring a moment of calm and reflection in the sparsely filled chapel space.

Anyone who organizes chapel services, let alone end-of-the-year ceremonies, knows how rare it is to find a moment of quiet and peace prior to the beginning of a service. Quite often participants are putting things in place, checking last-minute details, getting things organized, working out the anxiety of anticipation. Moreover, it is far more common for people to arrive late for services these days rather than early, given the hectic lives we lead. Showing up early to a service, leaving us with time on our hands, can make us feel at a loss as to what to do. "Shouldn't I be doing something more than just sitting here?" we ask ourselves. More likely, early arrivers would be outside conversing with friends or old acquaintances or checking last-minute messages on their cellular devices, and they may well have to be herded into the chapel so that the service can begin. Even odder to imagine is the possibility of lingering on in an empty space afterward. Normally we are on to other things, eager to move ahead with the schedule, not to mention feeling distinctively uncomfortable with the notion of lingering and taking in the moment. "Unlike our great-grandparents who passed the time, we spend it," writes Jeffrey Kaplan in an article on "the gospel of consumption,"[50] all the while acting more as tourists than pilgrims.

Above all, this photograph and the unique perspective it offered reminded me of two spiritual visions that ideally distinguish the life of an adult from that of a child or youth. First of all, it is the adult's capacity to "take it all in," to see the larger perspective of things rather than what young people are so likely to see—only a small portion of the larger picture. Futurist Bob Johansen wrote a book called *Get There Early,* which is not about getting to first base before everyone else does so to secure the competitive edge, but about getting there (in Johansen's case, his beloved baseball games) *early* in order to take in the fullness of the event, to see the ballpark fill up, to capture the tone and ethos of the assembling group, to watch it all develop.[51] Getting there early is, in his view, about sensing the fuller perspective, watching its evolution, giving ourselves time to be centered and prepared. If our lives are nothing more than moving frantically from one meeting to the next, from one event to another, then we lose that adult capacity to take it all in, something our young people desperately need to learn from the adults in their lives.

Second, I found myself imagining that the few people in that photograph were savoring the moment, taking it in for what it had to offer them. Perhaps some of those in the small gathering were alums, relishing for a few quiet moments the impact that chapel had had on their lives. Or perhaps they were parents or grandparents sitting there, waiting for their offspring to march in with the other graduates, and taking a moment to feel at a deeper level the power and poignancy of that particular milestone. It is the adult's ability to savor, to ruminate and relish an experience as it is taking place, to put it into context with the other experiences of life, that young people so need to see. As thrilling as it may be for young people to jump from one compelling experience to the next, they are nonetheless searching for something more lasting that will help them put their accumulated experience into context. Such models and signposts of understanding the richness of experience are unfortunately all too rare. As the historian Gary Cross writes in an important book on the delaying of adulthood among young men, we have produced "a culture of the infinite present, driven not by memory or anticipation but by thrills."[52] This is as true of adults as it is of young people. Thrills are the property and experience of tourists; pilgrims seek something more. While a child collects experiences and moves from one to another, a mature adult can bring those experiences together and relish them for their beauty, depth, and mystery.

This opportunity to reflect on the larger perspective is one of the reasons I love the important ceremonies that conclude an academic year or a young person's time in school or college. It is in such moments that we are likely to feel the mystery of time in all of its power, melancholy, pride, and relinquishment. Having been on the platform of many of these occasions, I have been privileged to see the expressions on the faces of parents as they take in the profundity of the moment, be it tinged with loss or pride. No doubt many are remembering experiences with their children that have led to this moment, encountering the disbelief we all feel when something important in our lives has passed by so quickly. Similarly, the looks on the faces of students being honored or about to graduate is equally telling: often they seem to be thinking, "This is really weird," as they move through the unfamiliar experience and wonder what will happen next. Words that capture what the young person feels at that moment do not come easily; powerful transitions are not easily understood by young people.

In his recently published novel, *America, America*, Ethan Canin's main character, Corey Stifler, stops and considers the passing of years, conveying as they do a sense of the fullness of what can be savored from it:

> What you aren't prepared for is the way children change your past, too. That's the thing. Everyone knows they change your future, but to see them in their innocence—in their cribs and then on their bicycles and then in their cars, at their soccer games and then their recitals and soon enough at their graduations and their weddings—to see them through all of that is to know that everything you have ever done, every act you've ever had a part in, has another meaning as well, and that it is both greater and more terrible than the one you knew.[53]

At such moments the difference between being an adult and being an adolescent is palpable. Young people are still accumulating; adults are more likely to be savoring. In some way, adults can understand and define what this means apart from the powerful feelings that are overwhelming the young. It makes it no less difficult for some, no less joyful for most. But a mature adult has the capacity to take in the fuller picture and make sense of it, and to savor what the moment in all of its depth and mystery has to offer. Cultivating the spiritual life carries with it the potential to sense, linger, taste, and digest the moments worth relishing in life, where we can see, from the widest and deepest perspective possible, just how full life can be and just how often our cups can overflow.

In my own life, my moments of savoring always carry with them a certain sense of regret—I know that all too soon I will have to move on, take care of business, and tend to the more immediate in life. Gazing on a painting, watching a sunset, experiencing an intimate moment with another person, feeling a sense of proud wonder as I watch a classroom discussion come alive and carry on with a life of its own, I am painfully aware that such moments cannot last forever. When Jesus is transfigured on the mountain top, the disciples are so moved by this radiant image that they want to build booths to freeze the moment and make it permanent. But the tragic tinge of savoring moments is their brevity, making it all the more important to tend carefully to the moments when we can experience them.

The practices and cultivation of the spiritual life give adults the maturity to be alert to such moments. Through prayer—particularly in times when we least feel like praying—we practice and cultivate an attentiveness to the power of moments. In the fleeting glimpses we catch of God, as we make ourselves available to God, we learn something of both the power and transitory nature of a given moment. This is a power that goes deeper than a tourist's encounter with God; it transforms us as we make our pilgrimage. In turn, we invite our children and students to taste of this activity of savoring. Nothing is more valuable for a young person to see than a parent, a revered teacher, or a role model being touched, perhaps even overwhelmed, by the density and fullness of a particular moment.

On the night of the 2008 presidential election, in the midst of great reveling and celebration of Barack Obama's victory, we also saw the tears of Jesse Jackson as he took in the fullness of what this moment meant to him and the many years he and others had given to the struggle for the full rights of people of color. This is what it means to guide the young to see that there is more than simply the thrill and frenzy of the here and now. "You'll know someday how I am feeling on this occasion," a father may say to his daughter on her wedding day, or a mother to her son as the unpacking in the first-year residence hall is completed and it is time for parents to leave campus. That "someday" speaks not only to the accumulation of experience that an adult possesses, it speaks to one of the most fundamental distinguishing marks between adult and child, and our culture needs to identify as many of those marks as we can. Thankfully, the spiritual vision can make such distinguishing marks all the more potent and present in our adult lives. It is what can make the notion of maturity rich, complex, and appealing to young people.

I find it hard to imagine not being a parent or teacher without some acquaintance with and practice of the spiritual life. Whether we marvel at the growth of a child and the rapid passing of time, whether we give it all up to God in moments of tension and uncertainty, whether we send them off into the world free of our direct control (just as God sends us out into the world with a love that has no strings attached), all of these examples lead me quickly into a realm I would call the life of the spirit. The spiritual life allows us to be truly affected by life, as opposed simply to "doing" life. It is that life that can equip us for the inevitable uncertainties and perplexities we will encounter as we nurture young people. It will also equip us with hope for the future even in the face of sacrifice, and in turn can invite and provoke young people to ponder the wonder and intensity of the adult life. Pilgrimage, it turns out, has a curiously appealing quality to it, particularly to the young.

conclusion

KNOWING THEM BEFORE THEY KNOW THEMSELVES

I am nothing, Lucy thought with woe, and I have taken on all of this as if I were God. But before she went to sleep, she wondered whether just this were not what you did take on if you chose to be a teacher...this, the care of souls.

—May Sarton's novel The Small Room

My friend Mark, who works with church youth groups, reminded me recently that Sam doesn't need me to correct his feelings. He needs me to listen, to be clear and fair and parental. But most of all he needs me to be alive in a way that makes him feel he will be able to bear adulthood, because he is terrified of death, and that includes growing up to be one of the stressed-out, gray-faced adults he sees rushing around him.

—Anne Lamott,
Plan B: Further Thoughts on Faith

OVER THE YEARS, I have heard many wonderful and extraordinary tributes that students have made to their teachers, pointing to their care, their holding them to high standards, and the degree to which these teachers would go out of their way to help them. Yet there is no more eloquent tribute I can remember than one given by a graduate of the school where I was working. As he spoke of the tremendous help his history teacher had been to him, not only in understanding the subject matter but in understanding where that student was headed in life, he explained, "He knew me before I knew myself."

There is no greater experience that any young man could have had than to have his life taken in and interpreted by an adult he respected. We grown-ups tend to forget just how confusing and frustrating life can be, and one of the greatest gifts we can possess is the capacity to lend some interpretation in return. I do not mean telling them, "This is just a phase you are going through"—I have never found any young person helped by such an observation. Instead, it has to do with what we see in them—their internal resources, talents, and gifts—and how we can help them to grapple with and ultimately understand what they are experiencing and where they are headed.

I suspect that history teacher served as both an artist and poet for his student. On the one hand, he painted a picture of his student that could then be given to him for the purposes of interpreting himself. So, too, he served as a poet in putting words to what was ruminating inside of the student. He was able to make some observations that made sense: "Yes, you're right. I just hadn't thought of it in that way," the student might reply. Or, in the words of one of my former students, enthused about the class she had just taken, "He put words to things I had been wondering about for quite some time but simply could not explain." As artist and poet, the adult has captured some of the essence of the young person, heretofore not yet completely put together. Hence, the young person has the experience of being known before she knew herself. Growing up and coming to know ourselves is, in part, about someone taking the time and possessing the wisdom to notice things about us. "Everything waits to be noticed," sings Art Garfunkel in one of his songs, and that is certainly true of our children as well as our students. They are, implicitly, waiting for us to notice things that they have not yet come to understand about themselves.

If that history teacher can serve, in some way, as a model for the adult that our society needs, what was it about him that helped him to give back to the student some of what he needed most? What allowed him that wisdom and perspective? What were the elements, in other words, that led him to be such an influential adult?

---

(1) An adult can see young people for
who they really are.

With young people leading increasingly compartmentalized and fragmented lives, the wise parent or teacher is one who seeks to see the young person in his or her totality. Not how we would *like* to see her, not how we see this or that part of her, but how she is as a person in her own right, distinctly different from us yet at the same time capable of being understood.

Andrew and Amy are close friends of mine who have always held out great expectations for their daughter, Angie. Both have led busy and pressured lives, with demanding careers and high intellectual standards. Their daughter was a tremendous blessing to them, and they delighted in her forthrightness and courage growing up. At the same time, it was also becoming increasingly clear to Andrew and Amy that Angie was not going to follow in their high-achieving footsteps. Rather, she gravitated toward fashion design, gifted artist that she was, and as her interest in pursuing that talent grew, her ability to persevere in the highly competitive high school she was attending waned. Andrew and Amy were tremendously supportive of Angie following her passion, yet I suspect they felt no small amount of regret that some of the hopes they might have had for Angie—attending a highly competitive college, perhaps leading to the type of careers they had pursued—were not going to be realized.

Angie went on to attend art college and moved into her own apartment with some friends. Andrew had not seen her for a few weeks prior to the day the two were to have lunch together. When his daughter appeared at the restaurant, Andrew was shocked to see that she had cut off most of her hair, what hair she had left was shades of orange and blue, and her outfit was unlike anything he had ever seen. As he dwelt in that awkward zone, where he had no idea what, if anything, to say, something amazing happened. "All of a sudden," he told me, "I truly *saw* her, and for the first time I saw her as a person in her own right. Not someone I wanted her to be, but who she really was—Angie."

Andrew credits his practice of Zen Buddhism as a tremendous aid in helping him to see his daughter in this way. It had opened to him an understanding and interpretation of life on its own terms, apart from his own projections. In turn, he was now able to see—truly see, for the first time—the daughter he so cherished yet had seen only partially for virtually every day of her life until now.

How easy it is to see our young people solely from the perspective of the roles they play—student, artist, athlete—as opposed to complete human beings. Likewise, how easy it is to see them only from the perspective of what we would like them to be: an extension of our own lives, a reflection of our own incompleteness, our own dreams yet to be fulfilled. Seeing young people in their own right is the first step toward helping them see themselves.

Josh Maravich, son of the famous Louisiana State University basketball player Pete Maravich, who had died prematurely, once explained why he was, in part, playing basketball for his father in the years following Pete's death: "I always wanted him to be proud of me," he explained, "I wanted him to see me."[54] Such is the wish of many young people regarding those who have had or are having an influence in their lives: they want to be seen.

---

(2) An adult is able to put his or her own life to one side.

It may be the parent who is either chronically absent or over-involved, who tells her problems to the child or won't take the time to listen to the child's problems. It may be the teacher who overly identifies with one or two students, or who cannot make a connection with students at all. Be it one extreme or the other, our biggest challenge as adults is to be able to set our own needs aside and attend to the child in front of us. We make our greatest mistakes as parents or teachers when we cannot separate our own "stuff" from the role we play.

Recently I heard the noted writer and speaker Parker Palmer make this remark: "Perhaps the greatest compliment I can give to someone is that they are 'grown-up.'"[55] By this Palmer meant that such a person has been able, through hard work and reflection, to hold on to the complexity of one's own life while separating it from the tasks required of mature adults. It is the capacity to sort out our own issues as human beings, including all of the disappointments and woundedness, as distinct from the relationships we cultivate with young people. This is not to say that the adult has "solved" the problems of her life or has ignored her own needs. Rather, the adult—the one Palmer would compliment as being "grown-up"—has the capacity to avoid bringing those issues into the role of being a parent or teacher or mentor.

It may well mean that in the heat of a conflict with a child or student, I stop and remind myself of what I am most likely to drag into this situation, which has very little to do with the child or student in front of me. Young people have a tremendous ability to "set off" in us all of the voices and fears of our own adolescence. The "grown-up" I think Palmer has in mind here is someone who is able not so much to eliminate those voices and fears, as to catch himself before they interfere with the needs of the young person.

I have also found this to be a particular challenge when I am prone to tell a student exactly what she ought to do about a particular problem. In that situation, I am most likely speaking out of my own experience rather than the experience of the student, and it is a very real human challenge to remember that those two worlds are entirely different. In working with parents over the years I have discerned that in those moments when a parent is most upset, disappointed, or angry about a son or daughter, chances are the world of the adult is intersecting and interfering with the world of the child.

There is true blessing and grace when we encounter and are helped by someone who is able to be the "grown-up" Palmer describes. I well recall an experience I had in the hours after I had met with the student leaders (as described in chapter four) and felt as if I had been a complete failure as a leader. In the aftermath of that meeting I called up my boss, who happened to be at home. I told him that I needed to speak with him, and could hear in my voice that something was wrong. He was gracious and compassionate enough to invite me over to his home for a glass of wine. I told him what had happened, how discouraged I felt at the comments I had heard from the students, and even wondered aloud if I was in the right position in the school. He was attentive and careful in his listening, and—perhaps most important of all—was not shocked by what he was hearing. He reassured me that I was doing the right thing by standing firm on a number of issues, but that such firmness would inevitably mean that students would react to my setting of boundaries and test my mettle. They needed my firmness, yet that would not mean they would not challenge it.

My boss was tremendously helpful that day, and able to focus solely on the matters I had brought to him. I was not surprised by his response; the fact that I called him that afternoon meant that I knew he was the type of person who would be responsive and understanding. What did surprise me, however, was what I learned a few months later. He had left me that afternoon with a wonderful reassurance: he paraphrased St. Paul's words about nothing separating us from the love of Christ (Romans 8:39). With those words he did reveal, ever so slightly, something of what had happened to him that very day. Earlier on the afternoon I had gone to see him, the Governing Board of the school had informed him that they felt it was time for him to step down as headmaster.

I was astonished by what he told me—in all the time I sat with him in his living room, there was no evidence that he had brought any of this devastating news into our conversation. How could a person listen so calmly to the woes of someone else, following such a blow? In the scriptural passage he left with me as I departed, he shared some sense that he spoke out of the unfolding disappointment he was experiencing, but nothing else that afternoon revealed that his attentiveness to my situation was compromised by what had happened to him.

Nothing in my professional life has had more of an impact on me than that. Here was a person crushed by news of his own, yet able to set that aside as he listened to me. All of us have, at some point or another, been the beneficiaries of the attention and help of these grown-ups, who somehow have been able to draw the distinction between the goings on in their own lives and the needs of the person at hand. It is influence born of wisdom and a great deal of self-understanding. Perhaps even a sense of duty as well:

this person in front of me does not need or deserve a response from me that is clouded by my own issues in life.

---

(3) Adults do not always realize the impact
they are having.

This may not be the final point I should be making in a book aimed at helping adults in their work with young people. However, in the end, any conclusions or advice must give way to the mysterious nature of influence. In our work with our children or our students, we just do not know the extent or depth of the influence we have. We may know we are having some type of influence, and we can hope that the nature of that influence is good; yet the exact shape of that influence, or the manner in which it most touches our children or students, must remain an essential mystery to us.

We will never completely know just how we have had an impact on our children or students. Chances are we will not know where and how they are taking us in, where our influence takes hold and makes the most difference. Much of this we take on faith. If we are lucky, we may hear something from a student or child that will give us a clue as to how we have managed to exert the type of influence that, down deep, all of us wish to have. Perhaps they may tell us, years later, of those pivotal moments that had a strong impact on their lives, or the extent of our ongoing influence on them. Fortunate are those parents or teachers who get to hear something of how their life and convictions have managed to leave their mark on the next generation. Otherwise, we are left with the hope, if not the conviction, that we *have* made a difference by doing what we can. Where those seeds we plant find fertile ground is not under our control. No doubt this is one of the reasons why so many adults underestimate their influence on the young: if there are no clear indicators, how can we have any idea of how we have helped them to grow and develop?

A number of years ago, I had returned home to Washington, D.C., after a long road trip. In checking my voice mail, I was surprised to hear from a former student of mine who had called to say hello. It turned out that this student, now married with children, had been sifting through a number of his belongings, and had come upon a briefcase that I had given him one day at school. As he told the story, he had come into my office when I myself was doing some clearing out and had filled a wastebasket with things I no longer needed. There in the wastebasket was an old briefcase, and he asked me if he could take it. I said of course. Years later, as he found that briefcase, he recalled the importance I had played in his growing-up years and decided to get back in touch with me.

I was touched by what he was telling me on the answering machine, and felt, once again, that such moments were the icing on the cake, so to speak, in this world of teaching. In the moments following, I recalled being of some help to this young man, both with the normal struggles of growing up and during the time when his parents were going through a divorce. Many of those moments came back to my mind, thanks to his telephone call. What I could not remember, for the life of me, however, was giving him that briefcase!

To be sure, giving an old briefcase to a student is hardly a sign of lasting impact. Nonetheless, it does point out the elusive nature of this influence: we hope we will leave our mark, and we may be able to trace signs of our words or actions making a difference in their lives, but the true nature and extent of that influence on the young are not ours to know.

Books, articles, and lectures about helping young people grow up so often leave us feeling guilty or inadequate. It is immensely difficult and tangled work. As Robert Kegan reminds us, it is easy to make children into adults or make adults into children "by not claiming our greater authority, competency, or entitlement to lead; or by suggesting that we should operate as peer-like confidants of our children apart from our roles as their parents."[56] Where we land in that treacherous but important gray area he describes is no easy thing to gauge. That does not mean we should not be thinking about it—how can a conscientious parent or teacher not think about it?! But all of this talk about maturity and adulthood may make the grown-ups among us, as well as the child within us, wonder if we have to leave our own childlike joys behind. Nothing could be further from the truth. As one writer put it, "Every adult is a junior high kid with wrinkles."[57] The child within us, or that part of us that seems "stuck" in adolescence somewhere, is not eliminated; instead it is joined in this mystery by what we owe to the next generation, which happens to be the very thing they most need. Thus do we find our place in the cycle of generations, in the mystery of something larger than ourselves, passing on life in its many and varied forms to those in our care.

NOTES

1. See Tony Dokoupil, "Why I Am Leaving Guyland," *Newsweek* (August 30, 2008).

2. Robert Evans, *Family Matters: How Schools Can Cope with the Crisis in Childrearing* (San Francisco: Jossey-Bass, 2004), 242.

3. Gary Cross, *Men to Boys: The Making of Modern Immaturity* (New York: Columbia University Press, 2008), 148.

4. Cross, *Men to Boys*, 41.

5. Madeline Levine, *The Price of Privilege: How Parental Pressure and Material Advantage Are Creating a Generation of Disconnected and Unhappy Kids* (New York: HarperCollins, 2006), 86.

6. Robert Bly, *The Sibling Society* (New York: Addison-Wesley Publishing Company, 1996), 237.

7. Sharon Daloz Parks, *Leadership Can Be Taught* (Boston: Harvard Business School Press, 2005), 193.

8. See the Parents' Guide at the NAIS website (www.nais.org). See also Catherine O'Neill Grace, "Family Ties: How Involved Should Parents Be in the Life of Their College-Age Child?" Middlebury College (www.middlebury.edu/administration/

midmag/archive/ 2006/fall/features/family_ties/). Matthew Futterman, in "Under Pressure," *Wall Street Journal* (October 4–5, 2008), cites the National Survey of Student Engagement in 2007 that indicated that 75 percent of college first-year students and seniors almost always took their parents' advice.

9. Erik Erikson, *Insight and Responsibility* (New York: W.W. Norton & Co., 1964), 131.

10. From a prayer for young persons, *The Book of Common Prayer* (New York: Church Publishing, 2007), 829.

11. Parks, *Leadership Can Be Taught,* 100.

12. Evans, *Family Matters,* 245.

13. For a discussion of the theory of the "U", see Peter Senge, C. Otto Scharmer, Joseph Jaworski, and Betty Sue Flowers, *Presence: Human Purpose and the Field of the Future* (Cambridge, Mass.: Society for Organizational Learning, 2004), 86–92.

14. See George E. Vaillant, *Aging Well: Surprising Guideposts to a Happier Life from the Landmark Harvard Study of Adult Development* (Boston: Little, Brown, 2002), 13, 62, 67.

15. Laurent A. Parks Daloz, Cheryl H. Keen, James P. Keen, and Sharon Daloz Parks, *Common Fire* (Boston: Beacon Press, 1996), 140.

16. See William Damon, *The Path to Purpose: Helping Our Children Find Their Calling in Life* (New York: Free Press, 2008).

17. This story was reported to me by Sharon Herzberger, Vice President for Student Affairs at the time, at Trinity College, Hartford, Connecticut.

18. Guy Treborg, "The Vanishing Point," *The New York Times* (February 7, 2008).

19. Quoted in Donald Capps, *The Decades of Life: A Guide to Human Development* (Louisville: John Knox Press, 2008), 65.

20. James Fowler, *Becoming Adult, Becoming Christian* (San Francisco: Harper & Row, 1984), 6.

21. Mark Edmundson, "Dwelling in Possibilities," *The Chronicle of Higher Education* (March 14, 2008): B10.

22. Gary Comstock, *Becoming Ourselves in the Company of Others: The Work of a Gay College Chaplain* (New York: Harrington Park Press, 2001), 96–97.

23. Comstock, *Becoming Ourselves,* 97.

24. Edmundson, "Dwelling in Possibilities," B11.

25. Margaret J. Wheatley, *Finding Our Way* (San Francisco: Berrett-Koehler Publishers, 2007), 210.

26. Robert Bellah, *Habits of the Heart: Individualism and Commitment in American Life* (Berkeley, Calif.: University of California Press, 1985).

27. See "Surveys of Students Challenge 'Helicopter Parents' Stereotypes," *The Chronicle of Higher Education* (February 1, 2008): A22.

28. Evans, *Family Matters,* 85.

29. James Fowler, *Stages of Faith* (San Francisco: Harper & Row, 1981), 71, 152.

30. Krista Tippett, *Speaking of Faith* (New York: Penguin Group, 2008).

31. Diana Chapman Walsh, *Trustworthy Leadership* (Kalamazoo, Mich.: Fetzer Institute, 2006), 7.

32. Paula Lawrence Wehmiller, *Face to Face: Lessons Learned on the Teaching Journey* (Philadelphia: Friends Council on Education, 1992), 6.

33. Erik Erikson, *Dimensions of a New Identity* (New York: W.W. Norton & Co., 1974), 124.

34. David F. Ford, *The Shape of Living* (Grand Rapids: Baker Books, 2004), 155.

35. Bob Johansen, *Get There Early* (San Francisco: Jossey-Bass, 2007), 52, 71.

36. Erik Erikson, *Childhood and Society* (New York: W.W. Norton & Co., 1963), 266–267.

37. Fran Norris Scoble, *Wisdom Observed* (Pasadena, Calif.: Westridge School, 2008), 128.

38. Henri Nouwen, *Reaching Out: The Three Movements of the Spiritual Life* (New York: Doubleday Dell Publishing Group, 1975), 36.

39. Johansen, *Get There Early*, 37.

40. Richard R. Niebuhr, "Pilgrims and Pioneers," *Parabola* IX, no. 3 (Autumn 1984): 6–13.

41. Willard Waller, Sociology of Teaching, as quoted by Sara Lawrence-Lightfoot, *The Essential Conversation: What Parents and Teachers Can Learn from Each Other* (New York: Random House, 2003), 30.

42. See Sigmund Freud, *Civilization and Its Discontents* (New York: W.W. Norton and Company, 1961), 62.

43. See Stephen Prothero, *Religious Literacy: What Every American Needs to Know—and Doesn't* (San Francisco: HarperCollins, 2007).

44. M. Shawn Copeland, "Saying Yes and Saying No," in Dorothy C. Bass, ed., *Practicing Our Faith* (San Francisco: Jossey-Bass, 1997), 65.

45. As quoted by Bellah, *Habits of the Heart*, 294.

46. Professor Mary Evelyn Tucker, Yale School of Forestry and Environmental Studies and Yale Divinity School, in an address to the New England Independent School Spiritual Council, meeting at St. Mark's School, Southborough, Massachusetts (November 2, 2007).

47. Richard Luov, *Last Child in the Woods* (Chapel Hill, N.C.: Algonquin Books, 2006), 298.

48. Madeline Levine, "Challenging the Culture of Affluence," *Independent School* (Fall 2007): 30.

49. Robert Coles, *Times of Surrender* (Iowa City: University of Iowa Press, 1988), xii.

50. Jeffrey Kaplan, "The Gospel of Consumption," *Orion* (May–June 2008): 42.

51. Johansen, *Get There Early*, 3–7.

52. Cross, *Men to Boys*, 255.

53. Ethan Canin, *America, America* (New York: Random House, 2008), 12–13.

54. See Mark Krieger, *Pistol: The Life of Pete Maravich* (New York: Free Press, 2007), 308.

55. From Parker Palmer's comments in the concluding plenary session at the Biennial Conference of the National Association of Episcopal Schools in Tampa, Florida (November 7, 2008).

56. Robert Kegan, *In Over Our Heads: The Mental Demands of Modern Life* (Cambridge, Mass.: Harvard University Press, 1994), 80–81.

57. Kenda Creasy Dean, *Practicing Passion* (Grand Rapids: Eerdmans, 2004), 2.

A GUIDE FOR REFLECTION

Questions for Parents and Teachers

Chapter 1
WHERE HAVE ALL THE GROWN-UPS GONE?

1. The author believes that our culture is experiencing a fundamental shift in our understanding of what it means to be an adult today. What signs do you see of this cultural shift in your children/students? in yourself? in the parents and adults you know? In what ways are adults today different from your parents or grandparents?

2. What images come to your mind when you hear the word "adult" or "grown-up"? Who have been the "adults" in your life? When do you feel most "grown up"?

3. What are some of the questions your children/students are asking you? What do these questions—or the deeper

questions behind them—tell you about the inner lives of these young people? What are they searching for?

4. The author notes that young people's "inner core cannot develop in a vacuum, as it needs models of inspiration and admiration." How do you as an adult nurture the discovery of the "inner core" of your children/students? When have you been able to model for a child/student what it is like to be your "true self"?

5. Who are the adults you have most admired in your own life? Why? What would you like your children/students to admire most in you?

6. As you look at our contemporary culture, what frustrates you about our collective resistance to growing up?

Chapter 2
LANDING THE HELICOPTER

1. What are some of the advantages and disadvantages of our ability to be so quickly and constantly in touch with young people today?

2. The author makes a distinction between "fusion" with our children/students and having an "influence" on them (p. 22). When and how have you experienced this distinction?

3. What excites you about being an influence on your children/students? What concerns you?

4. When are you most likely to "swoop in" or "hover" over your children/students? Why? Remember a time when you were tempted to solve a problem for a child/student, but did not. What was the outcome?

5. Which important "inner voices" from the past or present do you rely upon to help you solve problems or confront situations?

6. What are your children/students hearing from you, over and over? What will they remember best about your words or actions?

Chapter 3
IS FIFTY THE NEW THIRTY?

1. What are some of the images that you associate with adulthood? What did you swear, as you grew up, that you would never do when you were an adult? Do you do those things now? In what ways have you become more like your parents or adult models from your childhood?

2. The author describes influence as "possessing a set of adult characteristics, such as patience, perspective, a sense of what constitutes real success and real failure in life, an ability to see the irony in life, and even the occasional sense of being profoundly out of step with some of the values and practices of the young" (p. 51). Reflect on times when you have experienced these characteristics in your own life. How did they change you? When have you needed them but could not find them in the adults around you?

3. When have you served as a "speed bump" for your children/students? What are some of the ways you might "slow things down" for your children/students, in order to allow them to develop their sense of perspective and patience?

4. When have you served as a "deep sea diver," helping your children/students go beneath the surface and

identify what they truly need? How did you "see" what was really meant or needed at the time?

5. Think of a time when you made a decision or took a stand that made you unpopular with your children/ students. What did that experience feel like? How did you cope with the feelings? What was the outcome, in the long run?

6. How does it feel when you, as an adult, see yourself as "different" from your children/students? When do you feel "old" or "old-fashioned" in comparison with them? Reflect on a time when it was helpful to your children/ students for you to be "old."

Chapter 4
BEING WATCHED

1. When do you find communication with your children/ students truly frustrating? When do you find it wonderfully refreshing and enlightening?

2. Think of a time when you, as a teacher or parent, were "being watched" by a young person practicing the "art of studying adults." What did it feel like? What were you communicating to the young person by your words, gestures, moods, actions?

3. Where did you notice hypocrisy in your growing up years, when what adults said did not match what they did? How did you respond then? What do you think about those adults now?

4. When are you most likely to fall back on the adage "Do as I say, not as I do?" In what aspects of your life do you

find it most difficult to live out your convictions and deeper desires?

5. The author observes that "smaller things need to be taken care of before we are truly able to take on some of the larger tasks of life" (p. 74). When do you find it helpful to your children/students to "sweat the small stuff"?

6. What kinds of "support" for your children/students are you most comfortable offering to them? If you lean toward more soothing forms of support, how do you feel when you must challenge a young person to grow into more adult behaviors and ways of being?

Chapter 5
EMBRACING ADULTHOOD

1. What have been the biggest "surprises of adulthood" for you?

2. In what ways have you discovered that you are like, or unlike, your own parents or adult role models from childhood?

3. What are the most important lessons you have learned from adults who hurt or disappointed you?

4. The author writes that helping young people with the challenge of sorting out the essential from the non-essential is "a crucial task that only a discerning and patient adult can help them to do" (p. 88). Who helped you learn how to practice that discipline in your own life? How do you help your children/students to sort out what is most important in their lives?

5. When are you, as a parent or teacher, most likely to react in anger or shock to what a child or student has done or said? Why?

6. The author describes several values he has learned from young people, including time, absence, silence, a sense of occasion, and face-to-face contact. Which ones speak most powerfully to you? Which are the least appealing? Which would you like to learn more about?

Chapter 6
TOURIST OR PILGRIM?

1. In what ways do you feel you live "out of the box" compared to traditional notions in our society? When do you represent the traditional values your children/ students rebel against—the "box" they are happy to be "out of"?

2. What role did religion play in your life as a child? What role does it play in your life as an adult? How do you relate to religious institutions? Would you describe yourself as "spiritual, but not religious"? What spiritual disciplines do you practice? How do they—or the lack of them—help or hinder you in your life or work with young people?

3. How do your spiritual values inform and shape the decisions you make in your life and the way you relate to young people? How do they affect the choices you make and the boundaries you set?

4. Think of a time when you had to draw the line with a child or student. What was the experience like for you? What did you learn from it? What did the child/student learn?

5. What type of sacrifices or struggles do you worry are in store for your children/students in the years ahead? How do you help young people come to terms with failure and severe setbacks?

6. The author notes that "while a child collects experiences and moves from one to another, a mature adult can bring those experiences together and relish them for their beauty, depth, and mystery" (p. 119). Describe a time when you savored an experience, a milestone for a child or student. What was most satisfying about it? How were you able to share the moment with your child/student?

Conclusion
KNOWING THEM BEFORE THEY KNOW THEMSELVES

1. Reflect on occasions when you have been able to be an adult interpreter for your children/students, noticing things about them they may not have identified or articulated yet. How did you convey that knowledge to them? How did they respond?

2. The author tells the story of a parent who suddenly "sees" his daughter for who she is, apart from him and his expectations for her. Have you had a similar experience? What was it like? How did it change your relationship with your child/student?

3. When you are in the midst of a conflict with a child/student, what needs of your own are you most likely to drag into the conversation? What "buttons" do young people tend to "push" for you?

4. Recall a time when an adult was able to model for you the "grown-up" ability to listen with wisdom and compassion.

5. Who are some of the adults who had a significant impact on your life without their being aware of it? If you could contact them now, what would you say to them?

6. Reread the quotation from Anne Lamott's book *Plan B* with which the author begins the chapter. How could you be more "alive" in ways that might help your children/ students to "bear adulthood"? How could you offer a different vision of adulthood than of people who are "grey-faced" and "stressed-out"?